An Analysis of Fiscal Reform in Manipur

An Analysis of Fiscal Reform in Manipur

K. Jibankumar Singh

FORWARD BOOKS
NEW DELHI • GUWAHATI • VISAKHAPATNAM

FORWARD BOOK
4649-B/21, Ansari Road
Darya Ganj, New Delhi - 110 002
Ph.: 23263193 / 9811582579 / 09435116718
Fax: 011-23263193
Email: ektabooks@yahoo.com
www.akanshapublishinghouse.com

An Analysis of Fiscal Reform in Manipur

First Published 2012
ISBN 978-93-81763-04-9

PRINTED IN INDIA

Published by Akansha Publishing House, New Delhi and Printed at Harmain Offset, Delhi.

Contents

Contents

Preface

It is significants to mention that fiscal system refers to the mechanism through which financial resources for the Government and its agencies are procured, channeled or raised, and the scale and pattern of allocation of such resources is determined. In the State's fiscal system, the budgetary resources and expenditure through the annual budget constitute the fiscal system of the State Government. The Planning Commission determines the five yearly as well as annual resources and expenditure for development plans of the public sector as a whole.

Manipur is a state located in Northeast India. Though bestowed with beautiful landscape, ample natural resources by the nature, this state lags far behind in infrastructure and industrial development. The State has insufficient sources of finance of her own.

This book presents a categorical account of fiscal reforms in Manipur. Packed with facts and figures, this will serve the purpose of all those who are interested in public finance and financial management of government.

This work is the outcome of the findings of my project report for MBA (Finance) programme, submitted a the National Institute of Financial Management (NIFM), Faridabad.

I am deeply beholden to my mentors—Mrs. Anjali Anand Srivastva, Professor (Audit) & FA, NIFMA and Mr. H. Deleep Singh, MCS, Director, Institutional Finance, Government of Manipur for their scholarly guidance. Simultaneously, I am grateful to my seniors, colleagues and friends for their constant moral support, guidance and assistance. I am thankful to my family member for their encouragement and cooperation. Finally, I express my gratitude to Mr. M.P. Misra for undertaking publication of this book with meticulous care within stipulated time.

K. Jibankumar Singh

1
Introduction

The financial health of the Government of Manipur has come under increasing spotlight in recent years. The fiscal crisis faced by the State has been becoming more severe every year over the last decade. This has critically affected the functioning of the State machinery especially in the area of augmenting its outlays on physical and social infrastructure that are essential for raising of the State's economic growth. The delivery of public services as well as the operation and maintenance of the public assets have also been affected. The fiscal crisis in the State reached its peak during 1999-2000 with the fiscal deficit raising to 26 percent of GSDP and the turning of a surplus on the revenue account into a deficit during 1999.

A wide range of economic reforms have been initiated primarily since 1999-2000. This was by way of signing of a Memorandum of Understanding (MoU) between the State Government and the Government of India (GOI) on 19.4.1999 which was followed up by a second MoU on 20.6.2002 and the drawing up of a Medium Term Fiscal Restructuring Policy (MTFRP), 2000-2005. The debate about the critical finances of State Governments is continuing.

Generally all State Governments are suffering in some way or the other. The difference is in respect of the seriousness of the illness. The fiscal status of the Manipur is perhaps the most critical in the country. The disproportionate requirement for meeting expenditure for payment of salaries, pensions and debt-servicing is identified to be the main factor for the serious distortion. The frequent recourse to borrowing in the form of WMA and OD from RBI and GOI are indicators of the critical it's fiscal situation in the State. The determination may be appreciated from the fact that during 2001-02, the RBI suspended operation of the State's account for 329 days and which increased to 342 days during 2002-2003. In the context of Manipur "sustainability analysis is not so much an analysis of whether the present passive fiscal stance is sustainable or not, but more about how to restore sustainability ' (Ashok K. Lahiri, *A Study of State Fiscal Reforms in Manipur,* October, 2002). A crucial objective of fiscal reform in the context of Manipur is to eliminate the dependence on the WMA and OD. Overall improvement in the fiscal health of the State requires additional mobilization of resources in the least discretionary way expenditure rationalization and compression as well as effective utilization of Plan funds. More importantly, the State need to introduce effective collection mechanism of Tax and Non-Tax Revenue. Fiscal reforms have to be motivated by the overall objective of enhancing the State's potential for growth in the medium and long term by identifying areas with comparative advantage for the State and exploiting the opportunities emanating from the ongoing reform process in India.

State's Economy: An Introduction

Manipur, a small state with long history, is located in the extreme North East part of India. Pandit Jawaharlal Nehru once described Manipur " as a Jewel of India: for its scenic beauty. Due to its peripheral location and mountainous terrain, the State suffers from the obvious disadvantages associated with hinterland economics while pursuing policies for economic development. Manipur figures amongst the least developed States from their perspective of regional disparity. There is, therefore, a greater need for achieving higher growth rates to narrow the gap with the more advanced States. The structural features of the State have hardly undergone any noticeable change during the past years. The benefits from the Finance Commissions are found to be hardly adequate in the fiscal structure of the State. In the increasingly globalized economy it is imperative to establish strong links between the State's economy with the domestic and foreign markets. Achieving this, however, requires a firm commitment to fiscal discipline and prudent management of State finances. The era which commenced from the early 1990s provided a new set of challenges as well as opportunities for the State Governments. Paradoxically, benefits of such opportunities have been reaped by the advanced states, which have been able to respond rapidly to the emerging environment by undertaking policy and structural reforms. As a result, these better off States have seen higher investment and growth. On the other hand, the less developed States like Manipur have failed to benefit from such new opportunities due to a variety of reasons including its locational disadvantage. The percentage of fiscal deficit to the GSDP stood at 6.43% in 1995-96, 8.26% in 1996-97, 8.41% in 1997-98, dipped to 4.46% in 1998-99 but shot up to 23.03 % in 1999-2000, 8.03% in 2000-2001 and 10.30% in 2001-02. On the revenue side, the consistent record of revenue surplus was dramatically reversed since 1999-2000. The change in the outlook since 1999-2000 from revenue surplus to revenue deficit implies that prior to 1999-2000, revenue receipts use to cover a part of the capital expenditure but, since then, capital receipts are increasingly being used to finance revenue expenditure. The building up of public debt and the consequent interest liability have further fuelled the growth of revenue expenditure.

Topography

Manipur has a total geographical area of 22,327 sq. km. that is 0.78 per cent of the total land surface of India. About 90 per cent of the area is covered by the hills, whereas the remaining small area of 2,238 sq. km.constitute the valley. The State share its boundary in the Cachar and North-Cachar districts of Assam in the west, Nagaland in the north, Mizoram in the south. It shares an international boundary of 352 km with Myammar (Burma) in the south and the east. There are a number of rivers and streamlets in Manipur. The biggest river is Barak, which originates from the northern ranges of the State and join with Ganga-Brahmaputra System. The eastern half of Manipur lies in the catchment areas of the Chindwin-Irawadi system. Only 8.2 per cent of the total area is under cultivation, which constitute about 2.2 lakh hectare of gross cropped area. Hills, which constitute a large area of the State, are still heavily dependent on shifting cultivation whose contribution to total agricultural output is negligible.

Demography

The population of the State of Manipur is 23,88,634 as per census 2001 which constitute only 0.23 per cent of the total population of India and 6.2 per cent of the total population of the seven North-East States. The population of Manipur grew at the rate of 30 percent during 1991-2001 as against 29.30 per cent during 1981-1991, which was higher than the all India rates of 21.30 percent and 23.90 percent during the nineties and eighties respectively.

The State has nine districts, Chandel, Churachandpur, Senapati, Tamenglong and Ukhrul are the five hill based districts and Bishnupur, Imphal East, Imphal West and Thoubal are the four Valley based districts. Among the nine districts, Imphal West in the valley ranked first in terms of size with a population of 4.4 lakh. Around 27.30 per cent of the total population inhabit in the hills mostly by different tribes. The Meiteis, who account for nearly 63 per cent of the total population of the State reside in the valley. The population density of Manipur increased from 82 per sq. km. in 1991 to 107 per sq. km. in 2001.

The sex ratio improved from 958 females per 1000 male in 1991 to 978 in 2001. The State has a less adverse sex ratio than the country as a whole. The all India sex ratio was 933 in 2001. Manipur is relatively advanced in women's empowerment. Manipur's women are hard-workers who share the burden of the family with the male members and at the same time, they enjoy a good amount of freedom. "Meira Paibi" (Torch holding) the only organization of the women in the world participate in various activities specially at the time of violation of "Human rights" by the armed forces and other organizations. Markets run by women only, are common in Manipur. Among them "Ima Keithel" is the most famous market in the heart of the city.

Literacy rate increased from 59.90 per cent in 1991 to 68.90 percent in 2001, which was more than the all India average of 65.40 percent.

Human Development Index

The relative position of the State in terms of Human Development Index (HDI) (Table – 1.1) deteriorated from fourth in 1981 to ninth in 1991 (overall).[2] However, in terms of Gender Disparity Index (GDI)[3] (Table- 1.1), Manipur's performance is highly commendable as indicated by its relatively high rank (third rank), which remain unchanged during the period. The other important indicator of human development is the HPI (Human Poverty Index) , the value of which for Manipur was more than the all India average[4] in comparison to other States besides Mizoram (in 1981 and 1991) and Nagaland in 1981(Table 1.2).

Table 1.1

State-wise Comparison of Human Development Index and Gender- Disparity Index of North East States (1981 and 1991)

		Human Development Index 1981						*Gender Disparity Index 1981*	
		Rural		*Urban*		*Combined*			
		Value	*Rank*	*Value*	*Rank*	*Value*	*Rank*	*Value*	*Rank*
1	Arunachal Pradesh	0.228	28	0.419	24	0.242	31	0.537	28
2	Assam	0.261	26	0.380	28	0.272	26	0.462	32
3	Manipur	0.440	2	0.553	5	0.461	4	0.802	3
4	Meghalaya	0.293	20	0.442	21	0.317	21	0.799	12
5	Mizoram	0.381	9	0.558	4	0.411	8	0.502	18
6	Nagaland	0.295	19	0.519	8	0.328	20	0.783	16
7	Tripura	0.264	23	0.498	12	0.287	24	0.422	31
	All India	**0.263**		**0.442**		**0.302**		**0.620**	

		Human Development Index 1991						Gender Disparity Index 1991	
		Rural		*Urban*		*Combined*			
		Value	*Rank*	*Value*	*Rank*	*Value*	*Rank*	*Value*	*Rank*
1	Arunachal Pradesh	0.300	28	0.572	15	0.328	29	0.776	18
2	Assam	0.326	26	0.558	19	0.348	26	0.575	30
3	Manipur	0.503	7	0.618	12	0.536	9	0.815	3
4	Meghalaya	0.332	24	0.624	10	0.365	24	0.807	12
5	Mizoram	0.464	10	0.648	5	0.548	7	0.770	6
6	Nagaland	0.442	13	0.633	7	0.486	11	0.729	21
7	Tripura	0.368	20	0.551	20	0.389	22	0.531	29
	All India	**0.340**		**0.511**		**0.381**		**0.676**	

Source: Ashok K. Lahiri, A Study of State Fiscal Reform in Manipur, October,2002

Table 1.2
State-wise Comparison of Human Poverty Index of North East States

		Human Poverty Index 1981					
		Rural		*Urban*		*Combined*	
		Value	*Rank*	*Value*	*Rank*	*Value*	*Rank*
1	Arunachal Pradesh	62.03	31	30.04	25	59.86	32
2	Assam	60.19	28	33.37	28	56.00	59
3	Manipur	56.81	24	33.97	30	50.82	21
4	Meghalaya	60.64	29	23.43	11	54.02	26
5	Mizoram	54.39	19	29.62	23	47.97	18
6	Nagaland	53.80	18	25.70	19	49.37	19
7	Tripura	55.19	21	25.64	18	51.86	22
	All India	**53.28**		**27.21**		**47.33**	
		Human Poverty Index 1991					
		Rural		*Urban*		*Combined*	
		Value	*Rank*	*Value*	*Rank*	*Value*	*Rank*
1	Arunachal Pradesh	53.71	31	24.56	25	49.62	30
2	Assam	52.57	25	21.79	23	48.95	27
3	Manipur	47.49	20	26.22	28	41.63	21
4	Meghalaya	56.45	31	18.05	14	49.19	28
5	Mizoram	45.96	18	17.39	11	32.20	14
6	Nagaland	56.83	21	21.70	22	42.07	22
7	Tripura	49.54	22	20.37	19	44.89	24
	All India	**44.81**		**22.00**		**36.36**	

Source: Ashok K. Lahiri, *A Study of State Fiscal Reform in Manipur, October, 2002*

Note: The HPI is a composite of variables capturing deprivation in three dimension of human development, viz economic, educational and health. These have been captured by proportion of population below poverty line, proportion of population without access to safe drinking water.

Infrastructure

The development of other infrastructure such as energy, irrigation, communication, transport etc. and the facilities of marketing and banking lags behind other parts of the country. Owing to these infrastructure lags, the capital/output ratio is higher which is not attractive for private sector investments.

Transport

The State is linked to the rest of the country only through two National Highways. The railhead at Jiribam is limited utility because the wagon carrying capacity between Jiribam and Silchar (Cachar) is limited. Due to this transportation bottle-neck and due to the extortion by the terrorists who operate through these two highways, the prices of all products (import as well as export) including construction materials like steel, cement, bitumen etc. are higher than the other States of the country. Therefore, the cost norms of construction, operation and maintenance are also higher in the State and the availability of goods and materials is affected due to long haulage and problems in the intervening States. The density of the road compares unfavourably even in comparison with source of the neighboring States. In 1996, the density of road per 100 sq. Km was 48 Km in Manipur compared to 86.8 Km for Assam, 82.8 km for Nagaland and 140.4 Km for Tripura (White paper, 2002, Government of Manipur). The road coverage (road length per 100 sq. km) in the State was 23.8 Km/sq Km in 1981 which was lower than North East States, barring to 22.5 km/sq km for Meghalaya and 10.9 Km/sq Km for Mizoram. In the rural areas, the percentage of village connected with roads were higher than the all India average during 1991-92 to 1996-97, but it is still lower than the 100 per cent connectivity as obtained in Mizoram, Nagaland and Tripura.

Table 1.3
State-wise Comparison of Road Connectivity at Village-level in North East States

(Percentage of village connected by roads)

Sl No.	State	Population less than 1000			Pop. Between 1000 & 1500			Pop. above 1500		
		1991-92	1994-95	1996-97	1991-92	1994-95	1996-97	1991-92	1994-95	1996-97
1	Arunachal Pradesh	19.27	20.09	39.06	73.47	89.80	86.54	96.88	96.88	85.94
2	Assam	60.51	64.22	69.80	100.00	100.00	97.08	100.00	100.00	99.72
3	Manipur	39.49	40.23	39.26	86.36	91.82	65.83	98.80	98.80	89.82
4	Meghalaya	46.76	49.49	44.51	100.00	100.00	86.49	100.00	100.00	64.29
5	Mizoram	72.66	74.68	80.82	100.00	100.00	100.00	100.00	100.00	100.00
6	Nagaland	84.91	97.38	85.08	87.88	96.97	100.00	100.00	100.00	100.00
7	Tripura	74.59	79.51	48.13	72.34	85.11	100.00	100.00	100.00	100.00
	All India	36.52	37.45	49.18	72.32	76.54	74.58	89.82	91.72	78.04

Source: Planning Commission, as reported in Basic Road Statistics of India, 1995-96

Notes:

1. Road coverage refers to all categories of roads (both surfaced and unsurfaced) including National Highways, State Highways, Major district roads, other district roads and rural roads. Data as on March 31 of the indicated year.
2. Population base for 1991-92 and 1994-95 is 1981 Census and for 1996-97 is 1991 Census.

Industry

Industry is one of the key indicators of economic growth of a state or a county. The state does not have any major and medium Industry even after the completion of fifty-seven years of independence of India. In late eighties and nineties, most of the Public sector undertaking (PSUs) were established by the State Government except one i.e. "The Drugs and Pharmaceutical Industries Ltd" which is on 50:50 basis between the Centre and State Government. These PSUs are running into losses due to various reasons and are being planned for winding up. Handloom industry constitutes the nucleus of all manufacturing activity in the State and covers almost each household.

Power

The power supply of Manipur depends entirely on the share of power allocated from the central sector plants, namely, Loktak Hydro Electric Plant and Kopili Hydro Electric Plant in the North East region. Though per capita consumption of electricity in the State has been rising, the power generated experienced a sharp fall in 1997-98 to 6.8 lakh kwh from 38.4 lakh kwh in 1992-93. The power crisis in the State becomes acute during lean season when the production of power in the Central Sector Hydel Power plants plummets due to shortage of water. The installed capacity of power in the State has shown a marginal increase from 12,023 kw in 1991-92 to 12,622 kw in 1997-98. This could not meet the growing demand for power in the State notwithstanding tardy industrial growth and has led to a situation where the state has to purchase 99 per cent of its requirement form outside the State (Source: Economic Survey, 1999-2000, Government of Manipur).

The energy requirement estimated by the Central Electricity Authority (CEA) in its 16th power survey indicated that the state of Manipur require about 643 million kwh in 2001-02 which is estimated to increase to 857 kwh by 2004-05. The peak load was estimated at 156 mw in 2001-02 and it is projected to increase to 208 mw in 2004-05 (Table1.4)

Table 1.4
Energy Requirement and Peak Demand Projections by Central Electricity Authority 16th Power Survey- North East States

Sl. No.	State	Energy requirement (million kwh) 2001-02	2002-03	2003-04	2004-05	Peak load (MW) 2001-02	2002-03	2003-04	2004-05
1	Arunachal Pradesh	216	232	247	264	73	77	81	85
2	Assam	3669	3954	4237	4558	687	740	793	853
3	Manipur	643	708	780	857	156	172	189	208
4	Meghalaya	644	693	755	811	134	144	157	168
5	Mizoram	327	361	398	433	93	102	111	119
6	Nagaland	270	291	312	335	70	75	80	85
7	Tripura	635	695	760	832	161	176	193	211
	All India	529013	362572	597947	635065	85132	90510	96211	102161

Source: Centre for Monitoring India Economy, April 2002, Energy, page 129.

Irrigation

According to the All India Report on Agricultural Census, the gross cropped area was 2.9 lakh hectares which was reduced to 2.2 lakh hectares in 1990-91 out of which only 0.86 lakhs hectares was irrigated (White Paper, 2002-Government of Manipur). In reality, only a few thousand hectares of irrigated land have facilities for irrigation due to the geographical barriers in the State. The rivers flowing through the State dry up during the lean season. In short, the irrigation system in the State are wholly dependent on the Monsoons.

Communication

The communication system comprising of postal services, telegraph services and telephone services have had intense improvement only in the late nineties. There were 18,650-telephone connections in the State as on 31st March 1998, showing an increase of 15.5 percent over the previous year. The number of public call offices has also increased from merely 56 in 1990-91 to 1,134 in 1997-98 (Source: Ashok K. Lahiri, *A Study of State Fiscal Reforms in Manipur,* October, 2002)

Economic Performance

"Unlike most other States, Manipur has to grapple simultaneously with the twin issues of fiscal restructuring as well as restoration of law and order which have direct bearing on investment and growth" (Source: H. Deleep Singh: Medium Term Fiscal Restructuring Policy (MTFRP), Manipur 2000-2005, September, 2001, Finance Department, Government of Manipur).

The average real growth rate during 1980-81 to 1993-94 was 5.2 per cent per annum as per old GSDP estimates. As per the new series available from 1993-94, Manipur has achieved a nominal annual growth rate of around 13 per cent since 1993-94. Though the growth rate compares favourably with the all India average and other North-East

States, the quality of growth in terms of employment creation opportunities and sustainability has been unsatisfactory.

The share of agriculture and allied activities declined from 46.2 per cent in 1980-81 to around 40.70 per cent in 1993-94, whereas the share of secondary sector remained stagnant at around 11 per cent. The share of services registered a rise from 43 per cent in 1980-81 to 48 percent in 1993-94 (Source: Economic Survey, 1999-2000, Government of Manipur as per the old estimates).

Table 1.5
Growth of Annual Per Capita Income: Special Category States

(GSDP nominal at current prices)

Sl. No.	State	1993-94	1994-95	1995-96	1996-97	1997-98	1998-99
1	Arunachal Pradesh	9473	10238	12202	12177	13304	14781
2	Assam	6422	7298	7915	8416	9087	9863
3	Meghalaya	8343	8890	9857	10720	11692	12882
4	Mizoram	9390	9412	11520	12707	12817	NA
5	Nagaland	NA	NA	NA	NA	NA	NA
6	Sikkim	8555	9031	10756	12354	NA	NA
7	Tripura	5823	6030	7155	8455	8962	9514
8	Manipur	6804	6509	7835	10114	10456	10826
	India	8769	10068	11513	13121	14436	16537

Source: Demographic Composition: Hill Authority Act, Meiteis, Kukis and the Nagas, population as per 2001 census.

Manipur's per capita income of Rs. 6,804 which was well below the all India average of Rs. 8,769 in 1993-94 indicates that Manipur ranked fifth followed by Assam and Tripura among the seven northeast states at constant 1993-94 prices. The gap between Manipur and all India average has widened over the years. In 1998-99, Manipur's per capita income was 65 per cent of the all-India average compared to 78 per cent in 1993-94.

The era of economic liberalization that commenced from the early 1990s provided a new set of challenge as well as opportunities for the State Governments. Paradoxically, the advanced States which have been able to respond rapidly to the emerging environment has taken benefit of such opportunities by undertaking policy and Structural Reforms. As a result, these better off States have seen higher investment and growth. On the other hand, the less developed states like Manipur have failed to benefit from such new opportunities due to a variety of reasons (Source: H. Deleep Singh: MTFRP, Manipur, 2000-2005, Sept, 2001, Finance Department).

Emerging Challenges

In the Census 2001, the literacy rate of Manipur is 68.87% against the all India average of 65.38%. A large work force is therefore added to the State's economy that is not only literate but are professionals in many fields. There is a growing body of unemployment even in specialized fields such as medicine, veterinary, engineering, architecture, agriculture and in the new sectors of computer science and information technology. There is definitely a considerable scope for harnessing such a qualitative reservoir of human resources. The State has to develop policies to harness such talent into productive channels that would contribute to the productivity of the State and thereby raise the GSDP. If left untapped such talent could prove to be volatile and explosive.

With the onset of reforms at the national level since 1991, the role of the Government has been recast. In a market driven economy, market forces determine allocation of resources increasingly and role of Government has switched from being a direct participant in production and distribution to that of being a facilitator of private investment. Private investment flows to investor friendly environment. Most developed States have perfected the art of attracting investment with introduction of various incentives and concrete packages for investment. Manipur is a sub-optimal option from an investor's perspective owing to various factors such as the unfavorable terrain involving steep transportation cost, lack of natural resources having comparative advantages and poor infrastructure facilities etc. Tourism that has good potential is also stymied under the prevailing law and order situation. In fact, financial difficulties and law and order problems have become so intertwined that it has become difficult to comprehend as to which is the cause and which is the effect. Indeed a classic chicken or egg scenario.

The State is currently faced with the major challenge of providing infrastructure facilities conducive to industrialization particularly in the areas of Handloom and Handicraft, Food and Agro-based Industries and the emerging fields of computers, communication and information technology which have high value addition and low volumes. For this, providing improved infrastructure like better road connectivity and easy availability of powers are crucial.

Another area, which has a high potential for improving rural economy, is the development of irrigation infrastructure. The acreage under irrigation in Manipur in 1990-91 was 39.09 % of gross cropped area. The State has not been successful in completing the major irrigation projects such as the Khuga, Thoubal and Dolaithabi Multipurpose projects on account of mismanagement, shortage of resources, cost escalation due to delay as well as the prevailing security environment etc. Minor irrigation programme has also not taken off satisfactorily. Irrigation increases the gross acreage manifold, raises agricultural productivity and could significantly add to farm incomes. With proper watershed management and effective extension services on the choice of crops, better agricultural practices, ensuring timely availability of inputs, credit and marketing services etc., the agricultural productivity could be multiplied. The strengthening of rural infrastructure linked with higher productivity can lead to better forward and backward linkage between agriculture and industries, generate non-farm employment and reduce unemployment and poverty.

A sustained and respectable economic growth rate should be consciously targeted under the Five Year Plans and the

Annual Plans. In other words, the planning process will have to be professionalized and the allocation of resources carried out scientifically to achieve the target rate of growth. The practice of drawing up of Five Year Plans and Annual Plans should not be rendered ritualistic and sectoral allocations need to be determined only on considerations of achieving the identified developmental targeted rate of growth of the State.

The deficiencies mentioned in the above paragraphs have manifested in terms of severe shortage and poor quality of electric power, low levels of achievement in expanding irrigation potential and its efficient use, appalling conditions of roads, inadequate provision for investment in education and health facilities, poor state of urban infrastructure including water supply and sanitation. All these have been due to inadequate volume of investment by the Government in infrastructure as also ensuring proper utilization in the end uses. In addition to this, productivity of past investments by the Government in Public Sector Undertakings (PSUs) has not only been low but negative in many instances thus compounding the problem.

REFERENCES

1. The HDI is a composite of variables capturing attainments in three dimensions of human development viz, economic, educational and health. These have been captured by per capita monthly expenditure adjusted for inequality, a combination of literacy rate and intensity of formal education; and a combination of life expectancy at age 1 and infant mortality rate.
2. It indicates the deterioration of basic social services (education and health) in the State during the period. In 1981, the rural rank was 2nd and the urban 5th which has gone lower to 7th and 12th places in 1991, respectively.
3. The GDI estimated as proportion of female attainments to that of male for a common set of variables.
4. The Urban scenario was worse than the rural with 30 and 24 ranks respectively. During the year 1991, there was marginal improvement in rural side (20 rank) than in urban (28 rank) , however, the overall rank of the State remained the same for both the years (Table- 1.2)

2

Fiscal System in Manipur: Main Features

The Fiscal System

Fiscal system refers to the mechanism through which financial resources for the Government and its agencies are procured, channeled or raised, and the scale and pattern of allocation of such resources is determined. In the State's fiscal system, the budgetary resources and expenditure through the annual budget constitute the fiscal system of the State Government. The Planning Commission determines the five yearly as well as annual resources and expenditure for development plans of the public sector as a whole. Before discussing the fiscal sector reforms and trends in the next chapter, the important features of the State's fiscal system are discussed below.

Budgetary Parameters

The budgetary disbursement and receipts for the State Government budget are shown in Table 2.1. The estimates for budgetary transaction for the third tier of the Government i.e. Panchayats including Autonomous District Council (rural local bodies) are not yet available in necessary details. In any case, most part of the expenditure of the local bodies are run through grant-in-aid and there are covered in the disbursements given in Table 2.1. The important features of budgetary transactions for the State Government are as follows:

- Total disbursement form about 51.76 percent of the GSDP.
- Total receipts including borrowings account for about 40.53 percent of the GSDP.
- Revenue expenditure form about 40 percent of the GSDP.
- Revenue receipts constitute 35.62 percent of the GSDP.
- Capital expenditure form a lower position of GSDP compared to revenue expenditure, which constitute only 11.27 percent of the GSDP.

Table 2.1

Receipt and Disbursements of the State Government 2001-02

		Rupee in Crore	*% of total Disbursement / Receipts (respectively)*	*% of GSDP at current market price*
	1	*2*	*3*	*4*
I	**Total Disbursement(A+B+C)**	**1710.29**	**100.00**	**51.76**
A.	**Developmental (a+b+c)**	**1001.35**	**58.55**	**30.31**
	a) Revenue	791.23	**46.26**	**23.95**
	b) Capital	175.46	**10.26**	**5.31**
	c) Loans (excluding WMA)	34.66	**2.03**	**1.05**
B	**Non-Developmental (a+b+c)**	**550.87**	**32.21**	**16.67**
	a) Revenue of which	546.73	**31.97**	**16.55**

(Contd...)

	1	2	3	4
	Interest payment.	191.41	**11.19**	**5.79**
	b) Capital	—	—	—
	c) Loans and Advances	4.14	**0.24**	**0.13**
C	**Others (a+b+c)**	**158.07**	**9.24**	**4.78**
	a) Revenue	—	—	—
	b) Capital	158.07	**9.24**	**4.78**
	c) Loans(excluding WMA)	—	—	—
II.	**Total Receipts(A+B)**	**1339.20**	**100.00**	**40.53**
A.	**Revenue Receipts(a+b+c+d)**	**1176.78**	**87.87**	**35.62**
	a) State Own Tax	51.01	**3.81**	**1.54**
	b) State Own Non-tax of which	28.73	**2.15**	**0.87**
	interest Receipts.	1.00	**0.07**	**0.03**
	c) Share of Central Taxes	142.14	**10.61**	**4.30**
	d) Others	954.90	**71.30**	**28.90**
B	**Capital Receipts**	**162.42**	**12.13**	**4.92**
	a) State Provident Fund (Net)	15.16	**1.13**	**0.46**
	b) Recovery of Loans & Advances	0.47	**0.04**	**0.01**
	c) Plan Loans of which	118.72	**8.86**	**3.59**
	i) CSS/CPS/NEC	1.88	**0.14**	**0.06**
	ii) Internal Debt.	53.05	**3.96**	**1.61**
	d) Non-Plan Loans	3.65	**0.27**	**0.11**
	e) Share of Small Saving Collection(Net)	24.42	**1.82**	**0.74**
III.	**Overall Surplus(+)/ Deficits(-)**	**(-)371.09**	**(-)27.71**	**(-)11.23**
IV.	**Gross Fiscal Deficit**	**(-)340.31**	**(-)25.41**	**(-)10.30**

Source: Finance Account various issues, Govt. of Manipur and statistical Hand book

Deficit and Financing

The pattern of fiscal deficit in the State Government are shown in (Table 2.2)

Table 2.2
Levels of Deficit in State Budget

	As percent of GDP						
	1995-96	*1996-97*	*1997-98*	*1998-99*	*1999-00*	*2000-01*	*2001-02*
Gross Fiscal Deficit(GFD)	(-)6.43	(-)8.26	(-)8.83	(-)4.46	(-)23.03	(-)8.03	(-)10.30
Revenue Deficit (RD)	4.49	5.94	3.28	4.36	(-)9.95	(-)0.33	(-)4.88
Primary Fiscal Deficit (PFD)	(-)4.09	(-)3.99	(-)3.36	(-)2.48	(-)3.09	(-)6.73	0.91

Source: Finance Account, 2001-02, Govt. of Manipur and Statistical Hand book

Notes: GFD: Excess of total expenditure including loans (net of recoveries) but excluding WMA from RBI and Central Government over revenue receipts and non-debt capital receipts.
RD: Difference between revenue receipts and revenue expenditure.
PFD: GFD minus interest payments.
The term " Fiscal Deficit" in normal use refers to " Gross Fiscal Deficit (GFD)"

The pattern and sources of financing the deficits in the State Government and the Central Government Budget differ. The source of financing the deficit of the State is to borrow from the Centre as the State Government cannot borrow directly from other donors and the grant from the Centre.

The fiscal system has several important inter-linkages between the various organs of the government or public sector. The public sector comprises of:

- Government Departments

- Departmental enterprises and
- Non-Departmental enterprises.

Out of the resources raised by the State Government some are transferred to the State Public enterprises and local authorities following the 73rd and 74th amendments to the Constitution, the State Government have to form State Finance Commissions to determine the transfer of resources to local authorities. The transfer of resources to local authorities in Manipur require further streamlining the Second State Finance Commission has been set up in February 2002.

In deriving the financing pattern of a Medium Term Plan (five-year plan), it is the concept neither of Balance from Current Revenues (BCR) or Government saving which is nor of use. For the annual plan formulation, it is the budget support concept, which is directly relevant, and is therefore link to the Budget. While the Medium Term Plan is not finding a direct link with the budget on the estimates for the Medium Term Plan are prepared at some base year constant prices (2001-02 for the Tenth Five Year Plan). Whereas, all budget estimates are at current prices.

The Fiscal Federal System

It relates to the assignment of tax powers and expenditure responsibilities of the States and the consequent need of transfer of resources from the centre to the States. The Constitution provides for a system of revenue sharing arrangements. Besides, the Planning Commission (PC), Government of India also affect resource transfer under a well-developed system.

Budgetary Transfer

The current system of federal transfers in India provides for flow of the Central revenue to the States in segments, viz devolution of a part of the Centre's divisible taxes and grants-in-aid of revenue to States in need of assistance under Article 275 of the Constitution through the Finance Commission (FC), transfers through the Planning Commission (PC) in the form of assistance for State Plans, and other discretionary transfers. The statutory transfers also have several components, viz., tax devolution, revenue deficit grants, grants for Up-gradation and Special Problems, and grants meant for Local Bodies and Calamity Relief. Statutory transfers made up of tax devolution and grants under Article 275 account for a bulk of the transfers.

Some Changes for Statutory Transfers

Article 280(3) of the Constitution requires the Finance Commission to Make recommendation as to the distribution of the net proceeds of sharable taxes between the Union and the States and the allocation between the States out of their share in such proceeds. Formulation of principles that should guide the distribution of individual shares of each State constitutes a Central task of the Commission.

The Constitution (Eighteenth Amendment) Act, 2000 has altered the pattern of sharing of Central taxes between the Centre and the States in a fundamental way. Prior to the amendment, Taxes on Income other than Agriculture Income and Union Duties of Excise were shared with States under Article 270 and 272 of the Constitution respectively. The Act has substituted a new Article for Article 270 and omitted the old Article 272. The new Article 270 provides as under:

" 270(1) -All Taxes and Duties referred to the Union list, except the duties and taxes referred to in Articles 268 and 269, respectively, surcharge on taxes and duties referred to Article 271 and any case levied for specific purposes under any law made by the parliament shall be levied and collected by the Government of India and shall be distributed between the Union and the States in the manner provided in clause (2)"

(2) Such percentage; as may be prescribed of the net proceeds of any such tax or duty in any financial year shall not form part of the Consolidated Fund of India, but shall be assigned to the States within which that tax a duty is leveable in that year, and shall be distributed among those states in such manner and from such time as may be prescribed in the manner provided in clause (3).

(3) In this Article, " prescribed" means:

(i) Until Finance Commission has been constituted, prescribed by the President Order, and

(ii) After a Finance Commission is constituted, prescribed by the President by order after considering the recommendations of the Finance Commission.

The Finance Commission is now required to recommend such percentage of taxes and duties referred to in the new Article 270 that may be assigned to the States and also recommend the manner in which these may be distributed among the Sates.

Transfer to Local Bodies (third tier of the Government)

The operationalisation of the changes contemplated under the constitution requires action by both the Centre and the States. The pace of empowerment of these bodies to function as institutions of self-Government has, however, generally been slow (EFC, 2000).

A total grant of Rs. 1,600 crores for the Panchayats and Rs. 400 crores for the Municipalities is recommended by the EFC to be given to the State for each of the five years starting from the financial year 2000-2001 of which the grant of the State of Manipur is Rs. 18.77 crores for Panchayat including Autonomous District Council and Rs. 4.40 crores for

Table 2.3
Share of States in Allocation for Panchayats

States	*Share of States in allocation for Panchayats as per*							
	Rural Population (1991)	*Areas*	*Distance from highest PCI+ 0.5 s.d.*	*Revenue wrt own revenue of the State*	*Effort wrt GSDP*	*Index of Decentralisation Share*	*Composite Index for State's Share*	*Total for the State (Rs. Lakhs)*
	Weight= 40%	*Weight= 10%*	*Weight= 20%*	*Weight= 5%*	*Weight= 5%*	*Weight= 20%*	*%*	
Arunachal Pradesh	0.12	2.71	0.11	0.00	0.00	0.04	0.35	556.85
Assam	3.18	2.51	3.54	1.63	0.83	2.83	2.92	4668.95
Himachal Pradesh	0.75	1.79	0.76	0.12	0.10	0.89	0.82	1313.38
Jammu & Kashmir	0.94	3.25	0.87	0.00	0.00	0.28	0.93	1488.14
Manipur	0.21	0.72	0.20	0.00	0.00	0.19	0.24	375.43
Sikkim	0.06	0.23	0.06	0.00	0.00	0.04	0.07	105.85
Tripura	0.37	0.33	0.41	0.04	0.01	0.44	0.36	569.19
All India	94.37	88.46	94.05	98.22	99.06	95.30	94.33	150922.21
Total	100.00	100.00	100.00	100.00	100.00	100.00	100.00	160000.00

Source: EFC Report, 2000-05.

Municipalities. The amount shall be use for maintenance of accounts and development of in these areas.

Inter-se share of the States are based on:

- Rural/ Urban population of the States; 40%
- Index of decentralization; 20%
- Distance from higher per capita income, 20%
- Revenue effort of the Local Bodies; 10% and
- Geographical area; 10%

Due to non-empowerment of the Local Bodies to raise revenue by the State Legislation, the State has lost the share of 10 % from revenue effort during 2000-05 (Table 2.3)

3

Fiscal Reforms and Trends

Fiscal Reforms

Perhaps, fiscal restructuring was the most critical part of the macroeconomic stabilization and reform taken up by the Union Government after the 1991 economic crisis. The level of fiscal deficit combined both for the Central Government and State Government is more or less at the same level at the end of 1990's as it was at the beginning. Government debt is approaching a critical mark beyond which it could be leveled as unsustainable. Almost all the State Governments are facing hard budget constraints in providing even the basic minimum services through budget. Capital expenditure though has come down sharply.

After reviewing of the Economic Reforms in mid-1991, it was felt that the Indian fiscal system resulted in a slow and less satisfactory outcome. The complexity of the fiscal issues interlinked with all other macro variables, deeply entrenched systemic elements of administration, rigidities of expenditure, democratic constraints of unpopular fiscal and tax measures, and all the political uncertainties made fiscal reforms, the most challenging task for all shades of Governments notwithstanding a near consensus on the need of such reforms. The structural rigidities, therefore, continue despite wide-ranging reform measures.

Tax Rationalization

Tax rationalization process particularly for the indirect taxes was not only a matter of complex structure but also inter-linked to reform measures to be taken in other sectors like foreign trade policy, industrial policy, opening of the economy for foreign investment, financial sector reforms etc. The fiscal reform measures thus need to be sequenced aligned and restructured along with the reforms in all other sectors.

Administrative Structure

The complex and rigid tax administrative structure has to change with modern practices and even with psychology and spirit of reforms. Even the taxpayers lobbies could have interest in continuing with the same structure of discretionary concessions and ad-hoc benefits.

Rigidities of Expenditure

The allocations of budgetary expenditure in terms of contractual and obligatory payments like interest payments, pensions, defense, transfer to States, etc. have been growing in such a portion that there has been little scope of any sharp change in the allocation pattern of expenditure in the short period.

Democratic Limitations

It is well known that there remains certain basic issues, which no elected government would prefer to even raise. Taxing agricultural income, sharp reduction on food subsidy, downsizing of Government staff etc. are some such issues which no government has been able to face head on, howsoever, critical these may be for correcting fiscal imbalances.

Political Uncertainty

Political uncertainties, particularly, during the second half of the nineties was an important factor for delays in implementation of reforms so speedily required in a structure sequence.

States Fiscal Reform

It actually took long to realize, formulate and initiate fiscal sector reforms at state government levels despite the need for a well-synchronized mechanism for reforms.

Tax Reforms

The reforms during 1990s have been mainly guided by the report of the Chelliah Committee on Tax Reforms (1993). The main objectives have been simplification of the tax system, rationalization of tax rates, fairness in tax system, improvement in tax administration and above all providing a growth promoting tax structure. The wide range cf reform measures taken during the last decade include – in the case of direct taxes: moderation of tax rates, widening of tax base, incentives for development of infrastructure and housing and strengthening of enforcement, and in the case of indirect taxes: reduction in multiplicity of rates, rationalization of the rate structure, drastic reduction in the scope for discretionary changes and uniform floor rates for sales tax by the States. Further, rationalization and improvements in tax administration, of course, is a continuing process.

Disinvestments/Privatization/Public Sector Restructuring

The strategy towards public sector enterprises reform encompasses a judicious mix of strengthening strategic units, privatizing non-strategic ones through gradual disinvestments or strategic sale and devising viable rehabilitation strategies for weak units. The latest policy announced in the budget speech 2002-03 by the Finance Minister in Feb. 2002 as well as the recent years had the following as main elements:

- Restructure and revive potentially viable PSUs;
- Close down PSUs which cannot be revived;
- Privatisation;
- Industrial Restructuring;
- Capital Market;
- Reforms in Banking Sectors;
- Capital Accounts Liberalization;
- Bring down Government equity in all non-strategic PSUs to 26% or lower, if necessary; and
- Fully protect the interests of workers.

Systemic Reforms in Government's Borrowing Process

Though largely treading on financial sector reforms, the significant changes in the process of Central government borrowings to meet the budgetary deficits and temporary mismatches have been part of the fiscal sector reforms as well. Switchover to borrowings by government at market related interest rates, abolition of the system of automatic magnetization of the budget deficit, implementing a new system of ways and means advances, and developing as well as deepening government securities market have changed the whole system of financing the budgetary deficit and its relation with monetary policy stance.

The new system of ways and means advances (WMA), implies vacation of advances made by the RBI to the government with limits fixed for a given time period (ten days). This system has provided scope for a judicious credit creation, possibilities for monetary targeting, closer monetary and fiscal policy interactions, and mechanisms for open market operations to take care of surges in inflows of foreign capital. (Reddy, 2000b).

Notwithstanding the fact that greater reliance on market borrowings and bond finance (BF) and that too at market related rates rather than less borrowing along with monetization route, has led to an excessive debt burden for the government, empirical testing in a recent research study (Moorthy, 2000 June) has shown that move to market borrowings has been beneficial as:

(i) There is no evidence of a systematic shift to an unstable debt regime during the 1990s;

(ii) Reduction in monetization has helped curb the fiscal deficit by inducing a fall in primary expenditures larger than the rise in interest payments;

(iii) The decline in private sector interest rates due to the move to market borrowing indicates that overall costs of private borrowings are likely to have declined; and

(iv) There has been a surge in private investment relative to public investment.

Nevertheless, the study points out that Central and State Government finances are in precarious conditions due to large non-market debt, unfounded liabilities and contingent liabilities.

Expenditure Reforms Commission

To carry the process of reducing the growth in non-developmental expenditure, the government has set up (in February, 2000) an Expenditure Reforms Commission. The main terms of reference for the Commission are as follows:

- To suggest a road map for reducing the functions, activities and administrative structure of the Central Government.

- To review the framework of all subsidies, both explicit and implicit for maximizing their impact on the target population and minimize cost.
- To review the framework for determination of user charges of Departmental and Commercial activities: suggest an effective strategy for cost recovery.
- To review the adequacy of staffing under Central Government, Ministries, attached offices etc.
- To review the procedure for setting up of government funded autonomous institutions.
- To consider any other relevant issue concerning expenditure management in government and make suitable recommendation.

The Commission has already submitted to the government a few Interim Reports.

Fiscal Reforms Program for the States

Of late, several State Governments have been facing acute financial problems due to various structural rigidities as well as ad hoc compulsions including steep pay hikes to their employees. Specific time bound fiscal reform programs have, therefore, been discussed in the National Development Council (represented by the Chief Ministers of States) and with the Finance Minister. It was felt that joint effort on the part of the Centre as well as States is required to devise a medium term strategy for fiscal reform programs in the States. This strategy has taken the form of a package of advance financial assistance to be provided by the Centre to the States for an appropriate time bound reform program by signing a Memorandum of Understanding (MoU). Thirteen States have so far entered into an agreement with the Centre. These states are Punjab, Rajasthan, Himachal Pradesh, Manipur, Nagaland, Mizoram, Orissa, Sikkim, Uttar Pradesh, Madhya Pradesh, Assam, Andhra Pradesh and Jammu & Kashmir.

The main objective of the program is to wipe out the revenue deficit in the State budget in the medium term. The program components are:

- Reduction in Non Plan Revenue Expenditure, through appropriate taxation and expenditure measures and down-sizing of Government, where possible;
- Pricing/subsidy reforms, to reduce fiscal burden of the State and improve allocative efficiency;
- Institutional reforms, to improve regulation and efficiency in delivery of public services; and
- Reduction in the role of government in nonessential areas, through decentralization, disinvestments and privatization.

Recent Policy Initiatives taken by States to stabilize their Finances

The States have recognized the macroeconomic implications of the fiscal problem and some of them have in fact taken several policy initiatives to stabilize their finances. These measures, inter alia, include the setting up of Consolidated Sinking Fund for retiring public debt, the setting of ceiling on guarantees to place a cap on contingent liabilities and the establishment of guarantee redemption funds. The States of Assam, Karnataka and Maharashtra, Mizoram, Nagaland and West Bengal have taken initiatives for setting up of Consolidated Sinking Funds to help retire debt repayments. The States of Gujarat and Karnataka have prescribed limits on guarantees, while Rajasthan has proposed the setting up of a Guarantee Redemption Fund. As an important budgetary measure, States have begun to focus on expenditure management through setting up of Expenditure Reforms Committees. Some States have adopted decentralization as the main policy plank through which expenditure moderation would be achieved. Several States have initiated measures for reduction in non-merit subsidies, through better targeting and revision of user charges. On the resource mobilization front, States are at the stage for introducing VAT through an agreement to impose uniform level of sales tax. It is important to note that the financial health and management of State Level Public Sector Undertakings have been a cause for concern. To address this issue, Maharashtra has proposed to set up a Board for Financial and Managerial Restructuring. Finally, to enhance transparency in their budgetary practices, several States have published summary critical fiscal indicators in their budgets for 2000-01 along the lines of the documents entitled: "Budget at a Glance" presented by the Centre (RBI Annual Report 1999-2000, p 66).

The important policy initiatives towards reform as culled out from the Budget Speeches of the State Government Budgets for the year 2000-2001 and other supplementary information, classified broadly into fiscal consolidation, institutional and spectral reforms have been summarized in a recent RBI study (RBI, December, 2000).

RBI Initiatives on Reforms in State Finances

In response to the emerging new balances, it has been recognized that finances at the provincial level are critical to the realignment of the role of the state in the economy. Contextually, the Reserve Bank started a close and more intensive iteration with State Governments on a regular basis, and on a wide range of relevant issues. Accordingly, several significant initiatives have been taken during the recent years. (RBI, Jan., 2000).

- Reserve Bank in its role as adviser to the States, had examined the implications of contingent liabilities/ guarantees granted by the States to facilitate economic activities. A Committee of State Finance Secretaries has, with the active involvement of Reserve Bank, recommended limits on Government guarantees.

- With the support from Reserve Bank, a Committee of Finance Secretaries of State Governments is presently working on the issue of transparency and voluntary disclosure norms for State budgets.
- Recently, the States have also been encouraged to access the market for a part of their market borrowings. Within the approved borrowing program, the State Governments are provided with the option of raising resources in a flexible manner in terms of method, timing and maturates. The State Governments can borrow from the market from 5 percent to 35 percent of the approved borrowing limit under the new scheme. The State of Punjab, Andhra Pradesh, Tamil Nadu and Karnataka have raised funds directly from the market. The gains from the auction mechanism were seen from the fact that the auction based yield were below the preannounced rates.
- A Committee of the State Finance Secretaries is currently acting in an advisory capacity to oversee the indicators of financial parameters by the Reserve Bank.
- The Reserve Bank has been advising the State Governments in areas such as cash management, funds management and reforms in budgetary practices. Cash management techniques relate to updating of accounts, data analysis, technology improvements, updating of financial accounting and other codes and prompt analysis of monthly data. Modernization of budgetary procedures and financial practices and development of forecasting models or expert systems are some of the issues being examined as a part of reforms in budgetary practices.
- Mounting debt of the State Governments is increasing the burden on future generations. To achieve some

inter-generations equity, Reserve Bank has, in consultation with State Finance Secretaries, developed a scheme for Consolidated Sinking Fund, which is optional for State Governments.

Fiscal Responsibility Act

On December 11, 2000 the Government has introduced a Bill in the Parliament titled as "The Fiscal Responsibility and Budget Management Bill, 2000". The proposed legislation is to provide for the responsibility of the Central Government to ensure inter-generational equity in fiscal management and long-term macro-economic stability by achieving sufficient revenue surplus, eliminating fiscal deficit and removing fiscal impediments in the effective conduct of monetary policy and prudential debt management, consistent with fiscal sustainability, through limits on the Central Government borrowings, debts and deficits, greater transparency in fiscal operations of the Central Government and conducting fiscal policy in a medium-term framework and for matters connected therewith or incidental thereto.

The important features of the Bill, inter alia, provide as under:

(a) Laying before both Houses of Parliament, along with the annual budget, the Medium-term Fiscal Policy Statement, Fiscal Policy Strategy Statement and Macro-economic Framework Statement by the Central Government;

(b) Appropriate measures by Central government to eliminate revenue deficit and fiscal deficit and build up adequate revenue surplus;

(c) Elimination of revenue deficit by 31st March, 2006 and bringing down fiscal deficit to 2% of GDP in the same period;

(d) Prohibition of direct borrowings by the Central Government from the Reserve Bank of India after three years except by way of advances to meet temporary cash needs in certain circumstances;

(e) Greater transparency in fiscal operations and to minimization of as far as practicablc, secrecy in the preparation of the annual budget;

(f) Quarterly review of the trends in receipts and expenditures in relation to the budget by the Finance Minister and placing the outcome of such reviews before both Houses of Parliament.

(g) The Central government to cut expenditure authorizations in a proportionate manner, while protecting the " Charged" expenditure, whenever there is a shortfall of revenue or excess of expenditure over specified targets.

(h) Finance Minister to make a statement in both Houses of Parliament explaining any deviation in meeting the obligations cast on the Central government under this Act and the remedial measures the Central Government proposes to take.

(i) Relaxation from deficit reduction targets to deal with unforeseen demands on the finances of the Central Government on account of national security or natural calamities of national dimension.

Recent Trends in Government Finances

Trends in government finances in India continue to remain worrisome. The stabilization measures and economic reform initiatives taken since 1991 after the economic crisis had an encouraging impact in correcting the fiscal imbalances, particularly during the first two years. The trend, however, could not be maintained. Budgetary imbalances widened again reaching almost the same level towards the end of the decade, as it was at the beginning. Analysis of these developments has revealed dominance of structural rigidities in the Government finances, erosion of tax-GDP ratio over a longer period, virtual stagnation of non-tax revenue and higher growth rates in expenditure compared to growth rates in revenue receipts.

Basics of Structure of Public Finances

Before reviewing the trends in government finances in India it may be of use to first recall the basics of the structure of public finances in a country. These are best summarized in the Report of the Eleventh Finance Commission as follows:

> " The structure of public finances in an economy is defined by the level and composition of expenditure of the government (current and capital) and the instruments relied upon to finance them, viz the tax and the non-tax revenue sources and borrowings. The excess of government expenditure over current revenues and other non-debt receipts gets reflected in fiscal deficits financed either by way of borrowings from borrowings from internal and external sources or through seignorage, that is money printing. If expenditure persistently exceeds revenues, fiscal deficit, to the extent it is not covered by seignorage, steadily adds to outstanding debt, in the absence of commensurate increase in domestic savings, deficits in government budgets tend to spill over to the external sector in the form of current account deficit leading eventually to adverse balance of payments. This, in turn, jeopardizes the macro-stability, judged by stability of prices consistent with growth at attainable full employment levels. The solvency of the economy also comes under doubt. A restructuring programmed is called for to steer public finances away from such a spiral towards sustainable levels of debt and deficit."

Trends in Aggregate Budgetary Balances

Trends in different measures of budgetary balances both for the Central government and State Government as given in Table 3.2 for 1990s show that:

- The level of fiscal deficit in 1999-2000 combined for Central and State governments at 9.84 per cent of GDP was almost at the same level (9.64%) as in 1990-91, the crisis year. Latest available estimates (RBI, 2000, Aug) show that for 2000-01 (BE) the combined fiscal deficit level at 8.6 percent of GDP is significantly higher compared to the average of actual for such a ratio during the period from 1990-91 to 1998-99 which is 7.7 per cent.
- Fiscal deficit in the Central government budget for 1999-2000 (RE) at 5.6 per cent of GDP though lower, compared to the 1990-91 level of 8.3 percent is not significantly lower from any other year during 1990s except for 1993-94. Comparable estimates (excluding states share in small savings) show that the 1999-2000 (RE) level at 5.6 per cent of GSDP is higher than the average level of fiscal deficit during 1991-92 to 1998-99, which was 5.0 per cent (RBI, 2000 Aug).
- State governments together have a fiscal deficit of 4.7 percent of GSDP at its historical high in 1999-2000(RE) was above the average of 3 percent for the period 1990-91 to 1998-99.

Data and Reviews on Government Finances

Government finances being the key to macroeconomic stability remain under constant watch and review and exhaustive reviews on trends and current status are available periodically both from the government as well as RBI publications. It has been a welcome coincidence for this study to have an authentic and detailed review of government

Table 3.2
Aggregate Budgetary Balance: Centre and States

Year	Fiscal Deficit			Revenue Deficit			Primary Deficit		
	Centre	States	Combined	Centre	States	Combined	Centre	States	Combined
							(% Of GDP old Series)		
1	2	3	4	5	6	7	8	9	10
1990-91	8.33	3.28	9.64	3.47	0.84	4.31	4.32	1.69	5.00
1991-92	5.89	2.93	7.17	2.64	0.81	3.45	1.58	1.19	2.19
1992-93	5.69	2.92	7.38	2.63	0.72	3.36	1.29	1.06	2.23
1993-94	7.43	2.49	8.68	4.04	0.47	4.51	2.90	0.56	3.39
1994-95	5.99	2.86	7.36	3.22	0.73	3.95	1.42	0.84	1.93
1995-96	5.38	2.75	6.81	2.66	0.77	3.43	0.91	0.86	1.61
1996-97	5.23	2.97	6.82	2.56	1.43	3.98	0.57	0.97	1.35
1997-98	6.21	3.10	7.74	3.24	1.29	4.53	1.63	1.00	1.40
1998-99	6.80	4.47	9.50	4.08	2.72	6.80	2.13	2.34	3.23
1999-2000(RE/BE)	5.96	4.98	10.40	4.03	3.13	7.16	0.96	2.55	2.13

(Contd...)

1	*2*	*3*	*4*	*5*	*6*	*7*	*8*	*9*	*10*
							(% of GDP New Series)		
1993-94	7.01	2.35	8.19	3.81	0.45	4.25	2.74	0.52	3.20
1994-95	5.71	2.73	7.02	3.07	0.70	3.77	1.35	0.80	1.84
1995-96	5.10	2.60	6.44	2.52	0.73	3.25	0.86	0.81	1.52
1996-97	4.90	2.79	6.40	2.40	1.34	3.73	0.53	0.91	1.26
1997-98	5.87	2.93	7.32	3.06	1.22	4.28	1.54	0.94	1.33
1998-99	6.43	4.23	8.99	3.85	2.57	6.43	2.01	2.22	3.06
1999-2000(RE/BE)	5.64	4.71	9.84	3.81	2.96	6.77	0.90	2.41	2.02

Source: Report of Eleventh Finance Commission, June 2000.

Note: Old series for 1997-98 to 1999-00 have been derived from the New Series by using a conversion factor 1.0577. For 1999-00, FD and PD of the Centre exclude the States and UT's share of small savings.

finances in the Report of the Eleventh Finance Commission, (a statutory body set up every fifth year) published in June 2000 by the Government of India. One of the terms of reference of the Commission was to 'review the state of finances of the Union and the States and suggest ways and means whereby the governments, collectively and severally, may bring about a restructuring of the public finances so as to restore budgetary balance and maintain macro-economic stability.' This part of the chapter, therefore, draws heavily on the analysis and data given in the Eleventh Finance Commission Report as well as in Reports from the RBI.

A closer look at the different measures of deficit would reveal perhaps a more worrisome trend in that fiscal deficits are being driven more and more by deficits in the revenue account of the budget. Thus revenue deficit of the Central government, which accounted for about 40 per cent of the fiscal deficit in the budget in 1991-92, is now about 68 percent. Much more so in the case of state budgets, where the increase in revenue deficit to fiscal deficit ratio is from about 28 per cent in 1991-92 to about 62 per cent in 1999-2000. These trends simply show that the government is increasingly borrowing to finance non-asset creating expenditure from where no returns are expected. Further, the trends in primary deficit show that increasing interest burden alone is not the contributory factor in higher level of deficit. Latest available estimates indicate that the combined primary deficit in 1999-2000(RE) at 4.2 per cent of GDP was highest during 1990s except for the crisis year (1990-91) when it was 5.0 per cent (In table 3.2 it is low at 2.02 %).

Another important trend on deficits is the increasing number of State government with higher levels of deficit. Thus in 1999-2000, 13 out of the 25 state governments had faced fiscal deficit level of more than 7 per cent of their respective state domestic product, compared to 6 states in 1990-91, 4 states in 1995-96 and 8 states in 1998-99(Table 3.3).

Table 3.3
Frequency Distribution of States according to size of Revenue Surplus/ Deficit and Fiscal Deficit [as % of Gross State Domestic Product (GSDP)]

Surplus / Deficit (% of GSDP)	*1990-91*		*1995-96*		*1998-99*		*1999-2000*	
	RS/RD	*FD*	*RS/RD*	*FD*	*RS/RD*	*FD*	*RS/RD*	*FD*
Surplus	8	2	9	0	6	0	4	0
0 to –1	7	0	5	0	1	0	1	1
-1 to –2	4	0	7	3	2	1	7	0
-2 to –3	5	6	2	5	2	0	2	0
-3 to –5	1	5	1	10	9	5	7	8
-5 to –7	0	6	1	3	3	11	2	3
<-7	0	6	0	4	2	8	2	13
Total	25	25	25	25	25	25	25	25

Source: Eleventh Finance Commission (EFC) Report, June 2000.

The continuing precarious position of state government finances is also reflected from the latest available information that during 1999-2000, nineteen State Governments resorted to overdrafts with the RBI as against sixteen in 1998-99 and during the fiscal 2000-01 (up to June 30, 2000) eighteen State governments had resorted to overdrafts while two State governments could not clear their overdrafts resulting in suspension of payments by the RBI on their behalf.

Fiscal Reforms in Manipur

The present state of fiscal affairs in Manipur is both precarious and unsustainable. There was a precipitous deterioration in the fiscal health of the State in 1999-2000 with the fiscal deficit skyrocketing to 22.8 per cent of GSDP from 4.2 per cent in 1998-1999. The fiscal deficit to GSDP ratio came down to 7.4 per cent in 2000-01, but increased to 10.4 per cent in 2001-02(RE).

Table 3.4
Major Fiscal Variables

Rs. Crore

		1985-86	*1990-91*	*1994-95*	*1997-98*	*1998-99*	*1999-00*	*2000-01*	*2001-02*
	1	*2*	*3*	*4*	*5*	*6*	*7*	*8*	*9*
1.	**Revenue Receipts**	**227**	**390**	**592**	**864**	**898**	**1070**	**1045**	**1177**
	Own Tax Revenue	7	12	24	36	31	40	49	51
	Non-Tax Revenue	11	20	50	41	32	43	42	29
	Share of Central Tax	56	113	181	311	332	318	164	142
	Grants from the Centre	153	245	337	476	503	669	790	955
2.	**Revenue Expenditure**	**156**	**336**	**508**	**792**	**790**	**1356**	**1131**	**1338**
	General Services of which	42	103	187	275	292	561	516	549
	Interest payment	11	32	52	79	91	132	177	191
	Social Services	60	129	198	305	307	502	390	463
	Economic Services	54	104	123	212	191	293	225	326
3.	**Revenue Deficit(-)/ Surplus(+)**	**71**	**54**	**84**	**72**	**108**	**-286**	**-86**	**-161**

(Contd...)

1	*2*	*3*	*4*	*5*	*6*	*7*	*8*	*9*
4. Capital Receipts	**-9**	**78**	**63**	**192**	**109**	**657**	**234**	**340**
Total Borrowings (Net)(a+b+c)	**29**	**83**	**34**	**117**	**87**	**272**	**138**	**131**
a) Internal Debt(Net)	7	36	23	39	31	-80	28	46
b) Borrowing from Centre (Net)	17	34	6	59	49	64	19	44
c) Saving & Provident Fund(Net)	5	13	5	19	7	288	91	41
d) Recovery of Loans	1	1	1	1	0	1	1	1
e) Withdrawal of funds (Public Accounts net of Small Savings)	-20	15	16	-37	-39	120	-173	-154
f) Increase(-)/ Decrease](+) in cash Balance	-13	-17	12	-38	-137	264	137	396
g) WMA from RBI(Net)*	-6	-4	0	149	198	0	0	98
h) WMA from Centre(Net)*	0	0	0	0	0	0	131	-132
5. Aggregate Receipts (Net)(1+4)	**218**	**468**	**655**	**1056**	**1007**	**1727**	**1279**	**1517**
6. Capital Expenditure (7+8)	**62**	**132**	**147**	**264**	**217**	**371**	**148**	**179**

(Contd...)

1	*2*	*3*	*4*	*5*	*6*	*7*	*8*	*9*
7. Capital Outlay of which	**60**	**128**	**144**	**255**	**214**	**366**	**148**	**175**
Social Services	17	26	27	83	60	71	40	48
Economic Services	41	98	112	167	149	290	106	123
General Services	2	4	5	5	5	5	2	4
8. Loans & Advances by the Govt.	**2**	**4**	**3**	**9**	**3**	**5**	**0**	**4**
9. Aggregate Expenditure (2+6)	**218**	**468**	**655**	**1056**	**1007**	**1727**	**1279**	**1517**
10. Fiscal Deficit	**10**	**-77**	**-62**	**-191**	**-109**	**-656**	**-233**	**-339**
11. Primary Deficit	**21**	**-45**	**-10**	**-112**	**-18**	**-524**	**-56**	**-148**
12. Outstanding Debt of which **	**215**	**402**	**527**	**964**	**1249**	**1521**	**1928**	**2024**
Internal Debt	53	136	206	505	734	654	820	964
Centre	141	192	183	287	335	399	549	460
Small Savings & Provident Fund	21	74	138	172	180	468	559	600

Source: Finance Account, various issues, Government of Manipur

*WMA - includesWMA from Centre and normal WMA & Overdraft from RBI

** As on March 31 of the financial year

Table 3.5
Major Fiscal Variables (as percent of GSDP)

(Rs. Crore)

		1985-86	1990-91	1994-95	1997-98	1998-99	1999-00	2000-01	2001-02
	1	2	3	4	5	6	7	8	9
1.	**Revenue Receipts**	**48.8**	**42.9**	**42.2**	**38.9**	**34.4**	**37.1**	**40.0**	**35.6**
	Own Tax Revenue	1.5	1.4	1.7	1.6	1.2	1.4	1.7	1.5
	Non-Tax Revenue	2.3	2.2	3.6	1.8	1.2	1.5	1.2	0.9
	Share of Central Tax	12.1	12.4	12.9	14.0	12.7	11.0	6.2	4.3
	Grants from the Centre	32.9	26.9	24.0	21.5	19.3	23.2	30.9	28.9
2.	**Revenue Expenditure**	**33.6**	**36.9**	**36.2**	**35.8**	**30.3**	**47.1**	**40.2**	**40.5**
	General Services of which	10.5	11.3	13.3	12.4	11.2	19.5	16.5	16.6
	Interest payment	2.5	3.5	3.7	3.6	3.5	4.6	4.9	5.8
	Social Services	13.5	14.2	14.1	13.8	11.8	17.4	13.5	14.0
	Economic Services	9.6	11.4	8.8	9.6	7.3	10.2	10.2	9.9
3.	**Revenue Deficit(-)/ Surplus(+)**	**15.2**	**6.0**	**6.0**	**3.1**	**4.1**	**-10.0**	**-0.2**	**-4.9**
4.	**Capital Receipts**	**-1.8**	**8.5**	**4.6**	**8.5**	**4.2**	**22.8**	**10.5**	**10.3**
	Total Borrowings (Net)(a+b+c)	**6.2**	**9.1**	**2.4**	**5.2**	**3.4**	**9.4**	**5.9**	**4.0**

(Contd...)

1	*2*	*3*	*4*	*5*	*6*	*7*	*8*	*9*
a) Internal Debt(Net)	1.4	3.9	1.7	1.7	1.2	-2.8	2.6	1.4
b) Borrowing from Centre (Net)	3.7	3.8	0.4	2.6	1.9	2.2	1.8	1.3
c) Saving & Provident Fund(Net)	1.1	1.4	0.3	0.9	0.3	10.0	1.5	1.2
d) Recovery of Loans	0.3	0.1	0.1	0.0	0.0	0.0	0.0	0.0
e) Withdrawal of funds(Public Accounts net of Small Savings)	-4.3	1.6	1.2	-1.7	-1.5	4.2	0.4	-4.7
f) Increase(-)/ Decrease(+) in cash Balance	-2.7	-1.9	0.9	-1.7	-5.3	9.2	4.2	12.0
g) WMA from RBI(Net)*	-1.3	-0.4	0.0	6.7	7.6	0.0	0.0	3.0
h) WMA from Centre(Net)*	0.0	0.0	0.0	0.0	0.0	0.0	0.0	-4.0
5. Aggregate Receipts (Net)(1+4)	**47.0**	**51.4**	**46.8**	**47.4**	**38.6**	**59.9**	**50.5**	**45.9**
6. Capital Expenditure (7+8)	**13.5**	**14.4**	**10.5**	**11.7**	**8.2**	**12.9**	**10.2**	**5.4**
7. Capital Outlay of which	**13.1**	**14.0**	**10.4**	**11.4**	**8.2**	**12.8**	**9.6**	**5.3**
Social Services	3.7	2.8	2.0	3.7	2.3	2.5	2.7	1.5
Economic Services	8.9	10.7	8.0	7.5	5.7	10.1	6.7	3.7

(Contd...)

1	2	3	4	5	6	7	8	9
General Services	0.5	0.5	0.4	0.2	0.2	0.2	0.2	0.1
8. Loans & Advances by the Govt.	**0.4**	**0.4**	**0.1**	**0.3**	**0.0**	**0.1**	**0.6**	0.1
9. Aggregate Expenditure (2+6)	**47.1**	**51.3**	**46.7**	**47.5**	**38.5**	**60.0**	**50.4**	**45.9**
10. Fiscal Deficit	-2.1	8.3	4.4	8.6	4.2	22.8	10.4	-10.3
11. Primary Deficit	-4.5	4.8	0.7	5.0	0.7	18.2	5.5	-4.5
12. Outstanding Debt of which **	**46.3**	**44.2**	**37.5**	**43.5**	**48.0**	**52.8**	**55.8**	**61.3**
Internal Debt	11.4	15.0	14.7	22.8	28.2	22.7	21.7	29.2
Centre	30.4	21.1	13.0	12.9	12.9	13.9	17.1	13.9
Small Savings & Provident Fund	4.5	8.1	9.8	7.8	6.9	16.2	17.0	18.2

Though the fiscal deficit was eventually brought down to 7.4 per cent of GSDP in 2000-01 as per the revised estimate, the heavy dependence on ways and means advances from the RBI continued. In 1999-2000, for the first time, the surplus in the revenue account turned into deficit. The State entered into a Memorandum of Understanding (MoU) with the Government of India twice in the year 1999 and 2002, and a series of fiscal reform measures were undertaken, but mostly in the realm of expenditure compression, and very little in the area of garnering additional resources. These measures could not arrest the downslide, as the State's fragile fiscal health received a heavy blow from the recommendation of the Eleventh Finance Commission (EFC) that the

Commission have relied substantially on the past trends of expenditures of State Governments in different sectors following the normative approach and oversight the implementation of new pay scales during 1999-2000 following the Fifth-Pay Commission's recommendations. However, the overemphasis on the trends of actual expenditures has caused a paradox particularly in respect of resources starved state like Manipur. Because of Resource constraints, the State is not able to spend adequately, both for developmental and maintenance purposes. Assets created under successive Plans are not maintained properly. Flow of funds towards maintenance has been reduced to a trickle. Thus, the normative approach of the Finance Commissions which lays stress on trends of past expenditures under-assess our requirement for maintenance and have accordingly been awarded amounts which are embarrassingly meagre. The State is, therefore, caught in a low equilibrium trap. To illustrate, the award of the EFC for maintenance of Manipur State viz-a-viz the awards in respect of neighboring State may be seen below.

Table 3.6

Maintenance of Assets as recommended by EFC

(Rs. Crore)

Sectors	*2000-01*	*2001-02*	*2002-03*	*2003-04*	*2004-05*	*2000-05*
1. Maintenance of MMI	9.32	9.79	10.28	10.79	11.33	51.51
2. Maintenance for MI	2.47	2.59	2.72	2.86	3.00	13.64
3. Maintenance for Roads & Bridges	2.42	2.54	2.66	2.80	2.94	13.36
4. Maintenance for Building	9.42	9.89	10.39	10.91	11.45	52.06
Total	23.63	24.81	26.05	27.36	28.72	130.57

Source : EFC Report, 2000-05

Table 3.7
Comparative Outlay on Maintenance with Neighbouring Special Category States (2000-01 to 2004-05)

(Rs. crore)

States	*MMI*	*MI*	*Roads & Bridges*	*Building*	*Total*
1. Manipur	51.52	13.63	13.34	52.07	130.56
2. Nagaland	0.00	21.47	117.34	274.89	413.70
3. Meghalaya	0.00	29.82	210.55	167.04	407.41
4. Tripura	0.68	47.52	57.66	194.15	300.01
5. Mizoram	0.00	2.67	110.12	79.95	192.74

Source: EFC Report, 2000-05
MMI : Major & Medium Irrigation
MI : Minor Irrigation

The implementation of the Pay Commission's recommendations gave a final blow to the already fragile state of State finances. The root of the problems lies in the prevailing system of fiscal transfers between the Centre and States and inherent dynamics that gets built up in the process of Plan Financing and Finance Commission transfers.

As per the Gadgil Formula, 30 percent of the plan grants are earmarked for the Special Category States (SCS), which constitutes 5.3 percent of the total population, implying thereby seven times more per capita plan grants allocated to the SCS compared to the General Category States (GCS). Moreover, 90 per cent of the plan funds are being given as grants to the SCS. Notwithstanding, fiscal situation of the SCS is precarious today. The factors behind the failure of the SCS to translate higher plan allocation into higher growth are likely to be ineffective utilization of plan fund due to poor governance, near stagnation in the resource base and mounting expenditure liabilities associated with larger plan funds. These are also responsible for fiscal imbalances in these states. Plan financing increases the liability of the State even after the completion of Plan period in terms of interest due to higher borrowing, salaries and maintenance expenditure because of larger Plan size.

The Government of Manipur faces a chronic problem of shortfall in resources in financing even the committed expenditure. For example, in 2000-01, resources were available for financing only 65 per cent of the committed expenditure comprising non-plan salaries, pensions and debt servicing. This shortfall, which has been endemic since 1996-97, has led to the virtual postponement of operational and maintenance (O&M) expenditure and diversion of funds meant for Centrally Sponsored Schemes (CSS) and Central Plan Schemes (CPS). The changing financing pattern of government expenditure in Manipur clearly reveals the precarious nature of its finances.

The large fiscal deficit is reflected in an acute liquidity crisis and persistent dependence on ways and means advances (WMA) and overdraft from the Reserve Bank of India. Under Section 17(5) of RBI Act, 1934, the RBI provides WMA to the State Governments, to which it is a banker, to help them to tide over temporary mismatches in the cash flow of their receipts and payments. Such advances, according to the Act, are " repayable in each case not later than three months from the date of making that advance". There are two types of WMA : Normal and Special. Normal WMA are clean advances, while special WMA are secured advances provided against the pledge of Government of India dated securities. Since February 1, 2001, the Reserve Bank of India determined Manipur's normal WMA limit as Rs. 38 crore. From April 1, 2002, the limit for Normal WMA for Manipur was further increased to Rs. 50 crores. Strictly speaking, the balances of the States should not be overdrawn beyond their WMA limits and no unauthorized overdraft should emerge in their accounts with the RBI. However, under fiscal stress, like many other States, Manipur has been availing of overdraft from the RBI.

As per the Overdraft Regulation Scheme, in force from October 2, 1985, no State Government was allowed to run an overdraft with RBI for more than seven continuous working days. In case an overdraft appeared in the State Government's account and remained beyond seven continuous working days, the RBI and its agencies stopped payment on behalf of the State Government. The time limit for clearance of overdraft was increased from seven consecutive working days to ten consecutive working days with effect from November 1, 1993, further to 12 days effective from February 1, 2001 and effective from July 1, 2003, a State is entitled to a maximum overdraft facility of 100 percent of the normal WMA limit. The limit for bringing down the overdraft level within its permitted level of 100 per cent has been extended from 3 days to 5 days effective from February 1, 2001 and further extended to 6 days from July 1, 2003.

As per the White Paper on Manipur State Finance presented in June 2002, during 2001-02, the RBI suspended payments of the Manipur Government for as many as 329 days and 342 days during 2002-03. On average, thus, the Treasury was open only for three days in a month! In fact, the Treasury was fully closed for entire months in 2001-02 and 2002-03, and frequently the salary was paid on a bi-monthly basis/tri-monthly basis.

Manipur has been on overdraft from the RBI for several months of the year for quite some time. According to a RBI Report of 1998, in 1997-98, it was on overdraft for 118 days, and in parts of every month except in July and August, and payments were suspended for parts of March. According to the same Report, in the first six months of 1998-99, Manipur was on overdraft for 41 days, in all months except August and September, with payments suspended for parts of April and July. With all payments stopped by the RBI for days, the Government clears its overdraft and WMA with fresh receipts and immediately overdraws its accounts with the RBI, only to clear it again, overdraw its account, and so on. There was a pronounced deterioration in the fiscal situation in 2000-2001, when Manipur had to overdraw its account–far in excess of what is permitted–in the first five days of the RBI lifting its embargo on payments as the RBI stopped the payments in five days when it found that Manipur had exceeded its overdraft limit of Rs. 38 crores.

The acute stress in finances can be illustrated by the state of government finances in 2001-02. The year started with a negative cash balance of Rs. 442.33 crore, consisting of outstanding WMA of Rs. 41.83 crore and outstanding shortfall and overdraft of Rs. 400.50 crores. At the beginning of the year, there were hidden liabilities of Rs. 487.40 crore, consisting of Rs. 148.93 crores as deposits under Public Account for which matching grant were not available, Rs. 78.35 crores receipts from the Central Government for CPS/CSS/NEC which were not spent, Rs. 10.07 crores as backlog of the State's share for CPS/CSS, and payment arrears of Rs. 250.00 crores. In the preceding year, the revenue surplus projected- even in the revised estimates presented along with the 2001-02 budget- did not materialize. The revised estimate for 2000-01 had built in a Central grant of Rs. 200 crores, which did not come through.

The fiscal situation in Manipur needs immediate attention and corrective measures. As of September 8, 2002, the Treasury had been closed for a prolonged period with the overdraft having reached the figure of Rs. 557.64 crore as on April 1, 2002. Mounting instances of non-payment of salaries, diversion of development funds towards non-developmental committed expenditure, non-release as well as postponement of vital maintenance expenditure have started to seriously undermine delivery of public goods and services in particular and governance in general, thereby adversely affecting the development of the State.

The Government has been acutely aware of the fiscal problems and submitted a Medium-term Fiscal Restructuring Policy (MTFRP) for 2000-2005 to avail of the Incentive Fund created under the States Fiscal Reforms Facility established on the recommendation of the Eleventh Finance Commission. An empowered Monitoring Committee, comprising officials of the Government of India and the State Government, oversees the implementation of the MTFRP.

Insufficient State's Own Revenue

One of the major problems of Manipur is insufficient own revenue. Of the total expenditure of Rs. 1517.00 crores (Revenue + Capital+ Loans and Advances but excluding Debt Services) in 2001-02, for example only Rs.80.00 crores equivalent to 5.27 per cent, came from own tax revenue and non-tax revenue. Inclusion of Rs. 142.00 crores share of Central taxes in these calculations raises the measure of self sufficiency to Rs. 222.00 crore, equivalent to 14.65 percent of the total expenditure. Grants from Centre at Rs.955.00 crores financed 62.95 per cent of total expenditure.

Over the last one and half decades, the share of revenue receipts in GSDP has exhibited a tendency to fall by around 14 per cent points from 48.9 per cent in 1985-86 to 34.4 per cent of GSDP in 1998-99 and further reduces to 33.20 percent in 2001-02. The declining trend since 1998-99 has been endangered by a sharp fall in the share of central taxes and a gradual decline in grants. In fact, all the four components of revenue receipts has contributed to the fall through the share of own revenue constitute just around 35.62 percent of GSDP. Own tax revenue has remained more or less static at around 1.5 per cent of GSDP over the last two decades. Non-tax revenue, however, rose to 3.6 per cent of GDP in

1994-95 from 0.77 percent in 1981-82, before declining again to 1.0 per cent of GSDP during 2001-02. So the State's experience in collecting revenue under the two major heads of own tax and non-tax revenue has been frustrating in the nineties.

a) Own Tax Revenue

Erosion in tax-GSDP ratio over a long period of almost two decades and virtual stagnation in the level of non-tax revenue have been identified as significant contributory factors in higher levels of deficits in the government budgets, notwithstanding the relatively higher growth rates in expenditure.

Deceleration of growth in tax revenues: An analysis of trends in tax revenues by the Eleventh Finance Commission has shown that the buoyancy of tax revenue of both the Centre and the States which had been declining in the eighties, as compared to the earlier two decade went down further in the nineties (Table 3.8).

Table 3.8

Tax buoyancy: Centre and States

	Total Tax Revenue (Combined)	*Centre's Gross Tax Revenue*	*States' Own Tax Revenue*
1950-51 to 1959-60	1.38	1.38	1.39
1960-61 to 1969-70	1.16	1.15	1.17
1970-71 to 1979-80	1.30	1.27	1.35
1980-81 to 1989-90	1.14	1.15	1.12
1990-91 to 1998-99	0.96	0.91	1.04

Source: EFC *ibid.*

Note: Tax buoyancy refers to the change in tax revenue with respect to change in tax base (income). When it is one, tax revenue is buoyant; when more than one it is highly buoyant; and less than one is less buoyant.

With regard to gross tax revenue of the Central Government the trends show that between 1990-91 and 1998-99 the tax–GSDP ratio declined by 2.6 percentage points from 10.8 in 1990-91 to 8.2 percent in 1998-99. This is partly attributable to the change in the structure (Sectoral composition) of the real economy where the share of industrial sector has fallen and services sector has increased significantly without being brought in the tax- net in a significant way.

Some of the other features of trends in tax revenue are as follows:

Tax revenue, on an average, could finance about 60 per cent of the Centre's revenue expenditure during the eighties. The proportion during nineties, however, was about 55 per cent only.

Continuing reforms and rationalization of the tax structure have resulted in a structural shift in composition of tax revenue (Table 3.9).

A fall in the share of indirect tax collection from about 80 per cent of the total tax revenues in eighties to about 70 per cent in the nineties could not be fully compensated by the increase in direct tax revenue.

On the State's side, the dip in tax buoyancy occurred as revenue from sales tax, the principal component of their own revenue tax, showed a declining growth trend owing to tax competition among the States to attract trade and industry (EFC, 2000).

Table 3.9
Composition and Tax GDP Ratio: Central Taxes

	1990-91	1995-96	1996-97	1997-98	1998-99@	1999-2000 (BE
Tax Revenue as Percentage of Gross Tax Revenue						
Direct(a)	19.1	30.2	30.2	34.7	32.2	33.5
Personnel Income Tax	9.3	14.0	14.2	12.3	14.0	15.2
Corporate Income Tax	9.3	14.8	14.4	14.4	17.0	17.4
Indirect(b)	78.4	69.1	69.1	64.5	66.8	65.9
Customs	35.9	32.1	33.3	28.9	28.6	28.5
Excise	42.6	36.1	35.0	34.5	36.9	36.1
Tax Revenue as Percentage of Gross Domestic Product						
Direct(a)	2.1	2.8	2.9	3.2	2.6	3.1
Personnel Income Tax	1.0	1.3	1.3	1.1	1.1	1.4
Corporate Income Tax	1.0	1.4	1.4	1.3	1.4	1.6
Indirect(b)	8.4	6.5	6.5	5.9	5.5	6.0
Customs	3.9	3.0	3.2	2.7	2.3	2.6
Excise	4.6	3.4	3.3	3.2	3.0	3.3
Gross Tax Revenue #	10.8	9.4	9.5	9.2	8.2	9.2

Source: Economic Survey, 1999-2000.

(a) also includes taxes pertaining to expenditure, interest, wealth, gift, estate duty and VDIS for 1997-98 and 1998-99.

(b) Also includes service tax, # includes taxes referred in (a) & (b) and taxes of Union Territories and other taxes. Tax revenue figures for the year 1999-2000 are budget estimates and 1997-98 and earlier these are actual.

@ Tax database on Provisional unaudited tax figures as per Controller General Accounts.

Note: 1. Ration to GDP at current market prices for the year 1990-91 use old series base on 1980-81 and from 1995-96 onwards base on 1993-94 of National Accounts Statistics released by the Central Statistical Organization(CSO).

2. The ratio to GDP at current market prices for 1999-2000 is based on CSO's Advance Estimates.

Following are the some of the findings relating to Tax Revenue of Central Government and Sales tax revenue of States, in a recent study (Chaudhuri S., 2000b)

- Union excise duty collections have failed to keep pace with manufacturing output growth. The weakness has been in the system.
- The principal factor behind the fall in excise duty collections with respect to GDP is not tax policy per se, but the administrative mechanism of collection of the amalgam of compliance and of enforcement.
- The reason for the decline in customs duty with respect to GDP is quite obvious. The reduction in very high specific rates has not been fully offset by the combination of a steady depreciation in the external value of the rupee and the increase in the quantum (volume) of imports. It is unlikely that any reversal of the downward movement in the customs duties to GDP would be greatly reversed.
- The most notable feature of the movement of tax collections has been the steadily rising trend in direct tax collections – almost wholly made up of personal income tax and corporation tax collections. The annualized rate of growth for personal income tax in the period 1992-93 to 1999-2000 has been 17.8 per cent. The counterpart figure for corporation tax was 18.4 per cent. Given that the trend rate of growth of GDP at current market prices was 15.4 per cent in this period, the strong buoyancy for both the major direct taxes suggests enhanced collection efficiency of compliance and of enforcement.

Although the ratio of sales tax collection to GDP has not changed much, we do know that rate wars between States and competitive fiscal incentives have significantly eroded sales tax collections capacities in the States. The concordat mediated by the Union Government in November 1999 has resulted in uniform sales tax code and resulted in better collections in most States in the current fiscal year (2000-01). The agreement between the States has also frozen any fresh sales tax incentives to new investment, although incentives already granted would continue to be operative.

In the case of Manipur, the growth in the tax collection has not been commensurate with the growth of the economy as evident from the buoyancy estimates of the various taxes. Notwithstanding the State's effort at mobilizing more revenues through ARM and launching of collection drives, the share of collection drives, the share of tax revenue has been stagnating. Almost for all the taxes, the buoyancy estimates show a mark deterioration indicating poor performance of the tax machinery and an inadequate tax structure during the nineties compared to the eighties. Sale tax revenue which constitutes around 50 per cent of the State's own revenue, witnessed a marginal fall, while, for the period from 1981-82 to 2000-01, the buoyancy of own tax revenue is reasonably good at around 1.3. In the early part of the nineties, the share of sales tax in GSDP doubled from 0.5 per cent in 2000-01. The taxes, which suffered most during the nineties, are profession tax, land revenue, stamps and registration, estate excise duties and vehicle tax as evident from the poor buoyancy estimates.

Manipur's performance in tax collection has been considerably poorer than that of Assam (4.7 per cent in 1999-2000), Sikkim (3.5 per cent in 1996-97), Meghalaya (3.4 per cent in 1999-2000), and Tripura (2.5 per cent in 1999-2000). The factor for poor collection in taxes was prohibition, introduced from April 1, 1991 drags on State's finances by denying the State's sales tax, excise duties and license fees from bonded warehouses, wholesale and retail outlets worth Rs. 6 crore.

Table 3.10
Buoyancy Estimates of State's Own Taxes

State Taxes	*1981-82 to 2001-02*	*1981-82 to 1990-91*	*1991-92 to 2001-02*
Total Tax Revenue	1.30	2.29	0.61
Own Tax	1.03	1.15	1.06
Profession Tax	1.77	2.14	1.24
Stamps &Registration	0.12	0.56	-0.10
Taxes on properties	0.87	1.28	0.69
State Excise	0.62	0.97	0.52
Sales Tax	0.26	1.43	0.83
Vehicles Tax	1.28	1.05	1.11
	0.58	1.03	0.47

Source: NIPFP, report

The MoU signed between the Government of India and the Government of Manipur on April 19, 1999 envisage augmenting revenue from tax and non-tax sources. These measures were a part of a broader fiscal reform initiatives with the objective of reducing revenue expenditure and raising revenue and non-debt capital receipts to rein in debt levels, to ensure recycling of funds, and improve overall transparency and efficiency of governance. Earlier additional resource mobilization and austerity measures had already been introduced, although not with much success in particular, in the realm of additional resource mobilization. A second MoU signed on June 20, 2002 incorporated a Medium Term Fiscal Restructuring Policy (MTFRP) to strengthen and consolidate the reform measures.

Under the second MoU, sales tax being the major component of tax revenue, more personnel are to be employed for more effective collection of the tax. Redeployment of surplus staff to the sales tax department can achieve this goal without burdening the exchequer with additional salaries and wages.

It was reported that prohibition did not decrease the consumption of alcohol in the state. The consumption of India Made Foreign Liquor in Manipur has returned to the pre-prohibition level. In the year 1990-91, it was 996050 litres and in 1998-99, it was 977273 litres (Source: *Handbook of Manipur* 1999, page 317). It only denied the State its legitimate share of revenue and may even have led to criminalization of the liquor vending business in the hands of smugglers and counterfeiters. The Government has partially lifted the prohibition on July 30, 2002.

Reforms undertaken with respect to the revision of tax rate are as follows:

i) tax rates on Motor Vehicles have been revised with effect from April 29, 1999.

ii) Professional tax has been rationalized with effect from January 1, 2001.

iii) Rates of Stamp Duty and Registration have been revised with effect from August 16, 1999.

iv) Uniform floor rates of sales tax have been implemented from January 5, 2000.

v) Cinema show tax has been revised from Rs. 5 to Rs. 100 per show with effect from September 15, 1998.

vi) The Manipur Tax on Luxuries (Hotels and Lodging Houses Act, 2000) was notified on August 30, 2000 and Rules there under were notified on June 1, 2001.

vii) Hill Areas (House Tax) Act, 1966 has been amended from Rs.6/- to Rs.15/- per house.

viii) Taxes on Land Revenue have revised during 2003-04.

b) Non-tax Revenue

Non-tax revenue as proportion of GSDP has fallen by

nearly one percentage point from 2.5 per cent during the late eighties to around 1.5 per cent during the late nineties. The decline was mainly because of the less contribution of all services viz. general, social and economic services in terms of user fees. The revenue from Lotteries was one of the main sources of revenues which was reduced from Rs. 23.53 crores in 1994-95 to Rs. 1.67 crores in 2000-01 and almost 'Nil' in 2001-02. It is because of the banned on lottery in the State. There is a little hope to increase the revenue from lottery as it is started from first September 2003 and expected to earn at least Rs. 20.00 crores during the current year. The other major sources of revenue from Water Supply and Sanitation, Fisheries, Forestry & Wildlife, Power Tariffs etc. are far below the targets. With the State Level Public Sector Enterprises (SLPSE) in a bankrupt condition, dividends received were a meagre Rs. 120 in 1998-99 (Source: Finance Account 1998-99, Government of Manipur). The Non-tax Revenue from Power Tariffs at around Rs. 26.30 crores in 2000-01 to Rs.19.73 crores in 2001-02.

On the non-tax revenue side, the Monitoring Committee recommended that a system of indexation of water charges should be evolved. Similarly, in the Road Transport Sector, it recommended that bus fare should be linked up with an index of cost. In order to ensure satisfactory growth of the State's non tax revenues, the Committee further suggested that the State should examine the existing catalogue of all user charges and identify the areas where such charges could be be levied. In particular, the MoU said that the pending issues relating to water rates for irrigation, classification of land to contain undervaluation while registration etc. would be examined for finalization during the fiscal year 2001-02.

c) Share of Central Taxes

Share of Central taxes, after increasing seven fold from Rs. 56 crore in 1985-86 to Rs. 318 crore in 1999-2000, witnessed a drastic fall in 2001-02 to Rs. 164 crores , as a result of a reduced share of Central Taxes under the Eleventh Finance Commission's (EFC) award relative to the Tenth Finance Commission's (TFC) award. It is expected to rise to Rs. 206 crore in 2002-03 (Plan Finance 2002-03, Government of Manipur). Under the TFC, Manipur's share in Central Taxes, calculated as the weighted average of the shares of various taxes (excluding additional excise duty in lieu of sales tax), worked out to 0.006917 per cent. Manipur's share has come down to 0.00108 per cent (0.366 per cent of 29.5 per cent) of net proceeds of all taxes under the EFC award. However, under the EFC award, the fall in the share of Central Taxes was compensated by an increase in grants.

In contrast to the share of Central Taxes, grants from the Centre have sharply increased from Rs.153 crores in 1985-86 to Rs. 1108 crore in 2001-02. The increase in non-plan grants in 2000-01 pulled up the share of grants in GSDP from 24.6 per cent to 30.3 per cent.

As a proportion of GSDP, share of Central Taxes and grants from the Centre fell from 45 per cent in 1985-86 to 39.3 percent in 1990-91. The latest estimates of the share were 29.7 per cent in 2002-03(BE). On average, such transfers from the Centre constituted at least a third of GSDP in the decade of the 1990s. The erratic nature of such transfers – a decrease from 34.2 per cent of GSDP in 1999-2000 to 30.2 per cent in 2000-01, followed by an increase again in 2001-02 to 37.1 per cent and a decline to 29.7 per cent in 2002-03(BE) complicated the resource position of the Government.

4

Public Expenditure Management in Manipur

Introduction

Public Expenditure Management (PEM) is indispensable to achieve the objectives of State policy. Macroeconomic stability requires, among other things fiscal discipline i.e. expenditure control, growth and equity requires, among other things, optimal allocation and efficient use of resources including allocation of public money conducive to growth.

High levels of fiscal deficits could endanger macroeconomic stability. Substantial evidence exists that, in most cases, fiscal profligacy is the main factor behind high inflation, increase in current account deficit and finally sluggish or negative output growth. High levels of government borrowing (to meet revenue deficit in particular) can hamper growth of real economy by crowding out private investment. It generates upward pressure on interest rates and also reduces the amount of funds available for the private sector investment. Besides crowding out, the public sector investment/expenditure may provide less efficient outcomes compared to the private sector.

Governance and PEM

Governance encompasses the methods that societies use to distribute power and manage public resources and problems. It has been found that effective Governance is often the 'Mixing Link' between national anti-poverty efforts and poverty reduction. Even when a country tries to implement economic policies to foster pro-poor growth and mount targeted poverty programs, inept or unresponsive governance institutions can nullify the impact. Good governance requires adopting a policy framework that is responsive to the needs of the people. It also means efficient and equitable public expenditure management that results in appropriate investments in human resources, physical infrastructure and social protection.

To govern, according to an old proverb, is to choose. The choice is conditioned by political aspirations and concerns of economic realities. Once the choice is made, financial resources are allocated to achieve the underlying objectives. The choice and the allocation of resources are predicted on the performance or the outcome to be secured. The key actions of choice, allocation and performance form the heart of the process of the control of public money.

There are several ways in which good governance affects growth:

First, it has a direct impact on the effectiveness with which developmental programs are implemented.

Second, the quality of governance can help stimulate growth by making the policy environment more business friendly through deregulation, decontrol and procedural simplification.

Third, the general conditions for the law and order are a reflection of the overall level of governance and are particularly important for stimulating private sector investment.

The well-known 'four pillars' of governance is relevant to PEM as well. These are:

- ***Predictability:*** Lack of it undermines strategic prioritization, make it hard for public officials to plan for the provision of services, is an excellent alibi for non-performance to boot. This is needed as a signpost to guide private sector decisions in production, marketing, investment.
- ***Transparency:*** The IMF assembled in 1998 a 'Code of Good Practices on Fiscal Transparency', which covers: clarity of roles and responsibility, public availability of information, open budget preparation, execution and reporting, independent assurances of integrity.
- ***Participation:*** Needed for (i) sound formulation of expenditure programs; (ii) involvement of external entities; (iii) monitoring of operational efficiency and (iv) feedback.
- ***Accountability:*** For use of Public money and for the results of spending it, all accountability must be for performance defined as 'achievement of agreed results within the funding provided, without diluting their quality and respecting the prevailing norms of due process.'

PEM: Concept, Objectives and Dimensions

PEM: The Concept

PEM is an instrument of State Policy. It is part of the system of governance. There is a necessary distinction between the expenditure policy question of 'what' is to be done, and the expenditure management question of 'how' it is to be done. Thus the techniques required for formulation of expenditure policy are different from the techniques of using PEM as an instrument to implement the policy. The information and data requirement of PEM would be different from those required for policy.

It also needs to be recognized that PEM in principle, is an analytical framework that enables the state to diagnose and give prescriptions for remedial measures for policy. PEM is not a panacea for mismanagement of macro-economy and poor budget outcomes (JBIC, 2000).

Finally, there is no *one-size-fit all* PEM theory, It is only a technique. Like any other technology from water pumps to agricultural fertilizers to construction public expenditure ' technology' must be appropriate technology, in terms of (i) local factor endowments, (ii) local institutions, and (iii) real local needs (ADB, 1999).

Objective of PEM

Government collects money from the public in a variety of forms- taxation, rate of services, sale of assets and borrowings. The public in turn expects the provision of cost effective services, and more significantly, a prudent fiscal state of the nation. With the changing role of government, experience of the use of PEM technique in a large number of countries, and the ultimate purpose of state policy in view the objective of PEM illustrated in Table 4.1, have a universality about them (Premchand A. 2000)

Dimensions of PEM

Even though PEM is an instrument of state policy and is to be used to achieve specified objectives of the policy, it has over the period of use, become multidimensional. The different categories of objective to be pursued through PEM include:

Table 4.1
Objective of Public Expenditure Management

Effective Government	- Provision of services to the public within specified time and cost schedules.- Achievement of allocative and technical efficiency.- Ensuring that budgetary intent and outcome are congruent.- Matching outlays with resources.- Provision of management flexibility to the implementation agencies.
Responsive Government	- Achievement of macroeconomic stability- Responsiveness to changing economic situations.- Responsiveness to the changing needs of the client/consumer- Provision of a choice to the client/ consumer-Promotion of a utilization culture in lieu of spending culture.
Accountable Government	- Accountability for results- Provision of accurate information on the status of government finances.- Decision-making process to be transparent.

(a) Economic and Financial
- Macroeconomic stability
- Effective budgeting

(b) Management aspects
- Financial discipline
- Efficiency gains
- Program and project management
- Financial disclosure

(c) Public interest requirements
- Transparency
- Accountability
- Client orientation

(d) Political aspects
- Political acceptability
- Citizen participation.

In a PEM framework there are a large number of specific and alternate techniques, which can be utilized to achieve these objectives depending on the need, country specific circumstances, institutional capacity etc.

Ineffective Government Expenditure

As a Special Category State (SCS), Manipur gets 90 per cent of its plan size as grants and 10 per cent as loans from the Centre. Given its largely grant-in-aid character, government expenditure in Manipur should have a large multiplier associated with it, and it should result in a manifold increase in GSDP for a unit increase in such expenditure. Grants from the Centre and also the share from Central Taxes may be viewed as a net injection of resources into the State's economy, and should support vibrant growth in the State.

The absence of a consistent and robust relationship between GSDP and government expenditure is also borne out by the fluctuating share of government expenditure in GSDP. The share has tended to hover around 40-50 per cent excepting during 1999-2000, when the ratio jumped to 59.5 per cent. The proportion of per capita grants and share of Central taxes in the per capita income has witnessed a tendency to fall over the years from around 45 per cent in 1985-86 to 32 per cent in 1998-99, with a sudden jump to 36.8 per cent in 2001-02. However, this variation in net injection of resources in the Manipur economy does not seem to have affected its growth performance in any significant way. There are 4 (four) possible explanations of the absence of the ineffectiveness of the government expenditure in the State's economy.

First, a high import intensity of consumption, with a large proportion of both private as well as public expenditure being met out of goods and services bought from the rest of the country.

Second, leakages on account of corruption in the name of underground organization and vice-verse. Funds siphoned out through corruption results in actual expenditure being substantially less than the reported expenditure. Reported expenditure siphoned out through such unholy channels gets parked outside Manipur and fails to impart any impetus to either capital formation or to the growth momentum in Manipur.

Third, many of the projects taken up by the Government Departments in the fields of agriculture and allied services including forest and environment, industries, water supply schemes, power sectors, roads and bridges etc. could not be completed since a long time and those projects that were completed too are below the desirable levels. There are 328 (three hundred and twenty-eight) incomplete projects/capital works costing Rs. 25 lakhs and above as on March 31, 2002. The total original cost of these works is Rs. 392.15 crores and the revised cost is Rs. 1144.54 crores. The expenditure on these projects/schemes/ works as on March 31, 2003 is Rs. 643.76 crores (Source: Finance Account, 2002-03, Government of Manipur).

Fourth, the proportion of revenue expenditure in total expenditure is expected to rise from 70.8 per cent in 2001-02 to 84.5 per cent in 2002-03, while the share in total expenditure in GSDP falls from 50.4 per cent to 39.6 per cent during the same period. The shares of general services in GSDP has been rising mainly because of a steady rise in interest payments, with the shares of the other two components of revenue expenditure, namely, economic and social services remaining stable over time. The spurt in revenue expenditure in 1999-2000 was more pronounced for general services than the other two components. Since the early nineties, the shares of both social services and economic services have experienced a downfall by around 3 to 4 percentage points of GSDP (Table 4.2).

Table 4.2
Profile of Expenditure

		1985-86	1990-91	1994-95	1997-98	1998-99	1999-2000	2000-01	2001-02
									As percentage of GSDP
	1	*2*	*3*	*4*	*5*	*6*	*7*	*8*	*9*
1	**Revenue Expenditure**	**33.6**	**36.8**	**36.2**	**35.8**	**30.3**	**46.9**	**35.6**	**31.7**
A.	Social Service of Which	13.5	14.1	14.1	13.8	11.8	17.6	12.6	11.6
	Education, Sports, Arts & Culture	8.5	9.1	9.4	9.1	7.2	11.6	8.5	8.7
	Health and Family Welfare	2.2	2.1	2.0	2.1	1.8	2.6	2.1	2.1
	Social Security and Welfare	1.7	0.6	0.8	0.9	0.9	1.0	0.8	0.8
B.	Economic Services	9.6	11.4	8.8	9.6	7.3	9.9	6.7	8.4
	Agriculture and Allied Activities	3.9	4.6	3.5	3.1	2.6	4.1	2.4	2.8
	Rural Development	—	0.9	0.8	0.8	0.8	0.9	0.4	0.8
	Energy	2.2	2.9	1.4	3.1	1.6	1.1	1.5	3.0
	Industries and Minerals	0.9	0.8	1.1	0.9	0.6	1.1	0.8	0.9
	Transport and Communication	0.5	0.3	0.7	0.3	0.5	0.9	0.6	0.9

(Contd...)

	1	2	3	4	5	6	7	8	9
C.	General Services of which	10.5	11.3	13.3	12.4	11.2	19.4	16.3	11.7
	Administrative Services	6.4	5.8	6.4	5.3	4.8	8.2	5.6	6.0
	Interest Payment	2.5	3.5	3.7	3.6	3.5	4.6	5.6	5.8
2	**Capital Expenditure(3+4)**	**13.4**	**14.4**	**10.4**	**11.8**	**8.2**	**12.7**	**4.7**	**5.2**
3	Capital Outlay	13.0	14.0	10.3	11.5	8.2	12.6	4.7	5.2
	Social and Community Services	3.7	2.8	2.0	3.7	2.3	2.5	1.3	1.5
	Economic Services	8.9	10.7	8.0	7.5	5.7	10.0	3.3	3.7
4	Net Loans and Advance by the Govt.	0.4	0.4	0.1	0.3	—	0.1	—	0.0
5	**Agrigate Expenditure(1+2)**	**47.0**	**51.2**	**46.6**	**47.6**	**38.5**	**59.6**	**40.3**	**36.9**

Source: Finance Account and Statistical Hand Book, Govt. of Manipur.

Capital outlay as a proportion of GSDP has been highly volatile in Manipur. It declined from 13 per cent in 1985-86 to 8.2 percent in 1998-99, to rise again to 12.7 per cent in 1999-2000. The share fell nearly 8 percentage points in the next year. The share rose again in 2001-02 to 9.6 per cent (RE), and is budget to decline to 5.7 per cent in 2002-03.

Fifth, the committed expenditure such as wages, salaries, pension and other retirement benefits, interest payment and debt service payments exceed the total sum of State's own revenues, share of central taxes and non-plan grants. The Balance From Revenue was negative in 1995-96 at around (-) Rs. 66.6 crores which worsen steadily to (-) Rs. 358 crores in 2000-01.

The budget estimate for 2002-03 shows a further deterioration. Not only was there nothing left for Operation & Maintenance and other contingent expenditure, but, in order to meet this gap, the State Government had to divert funds released under other specified purposes such as CSS and CPS as well as the State had to borrow for plan expenditure and also to bridge the negative BCR.

The pressure of committed expenditure is also illustrated by the fact that nearly 91 per cent of the pre-actual non-plan revenue expenditure of Rs. 935 crores in 2000-01, had to be kept aside for paying salaries (non-plan), pensions and interest payments. The preponderance of committed expenditure in non-plan expenditure restricts the compression maneuverability of non-plan expenditure.

The State Level Public Sector Enterprises

i) The State Level Public Sector Enterprises (SLPSE) in Manipur are either running losses or closed down for a long time. Apart from poor management and faulty planning of the units that plague SLPE in many States as well as at the Centre, the very backward nature of

Table 4.3
Balance From Current Revenue

(Rs. crores)

	1995-96	1996-97	1997-97	1998-99	1999-2000	2000-01	2001-02
1. State's Own Tax Revenue	27.90	31.18	35.72	30.74	39.95	49.06	51.01
2. Share in Central Taxes & Duties	165.81	231.92	310.82	331.68	317.94	163.52	142.14
3. State's Own Non-Tax Revenue.	45.50	53.30	40.57	31.52	42.65	41.64	28.73
4. Non-Plan Grants (Including FC)	160.90	139.58	57.41	52.62	17.59	351.86	499.83
5. Non-Plan Revenue Expenditure	466.78	537.86	605.70	608.39	1089.59	935.28	1139.21
6. Non-Plan Support to PSUs	0.06	0.07	0.00	0.00	0.00	0.00	0.00
BCR(1+2+3+4-5+6)	**-66.61**	**-81.81**	**-161.18**	**-161.83**	**-671.46**	**-329.2**	**-417.5**

Source: Finance Account, various issues, Government of Manipur

the State in terms of poor infrastructure and communication is another reason for this poor state of affairs. With the MoU signed between the Government of India and the State Government during 2002, the State Government has decided to retain the following 5 PSUs out of 15 (fifteen) PSUs in view of their importance in the State's economy and their capability of managing without or with little Government assistance: -

a. Manipur Electronics Development Corporation Ltd. (MANITRON)

b. Manipur Police Housing Corporation Ltd. (MPHC)

c. Manipur Handloom & Handicraft Development Corporation Ltd. (MHHDC)

d. Manipur Tribal Development Corporation Ltd.(MTDC).

e. Manipur Film Development Corporation Ltd. (MFDC).

Proposal for retrenchment have been received in respect of 10 (ten) PSUs:

a) Manipur Cement Ltd.

b) Manipur Cycle Corpn. Ltd.

c) Manipur Pulp & Allied Products Ltd.

d) Manipur Food Industries Corpn. Ltd.

e) Manipur Spinning Mills Ltd.

f) Manipur Drugs & Pharmaceuticals Ltd.

g) Manipur Industrial Corpn. Ltd.

h) MSRTC.

i) Manipur Agro Industries Corpn Ltd.

j) Manipur Plantation Crops Corpn Ltd.

1092 employees are involved and estimated compensation/ severance package is Rs. 2870.47 lakhs.

VRS has been taken by the employees of 3 (three) corporations:

k) Manipur Electronics Dev. Corpn Ltd.

l) Manipur Handloom & Handicrafts Dev. Corpn Ltd.

m) Manipur Pulp & Allied Products Ltd.

147 employees are involved at an estimated cost of Rs 787.84 lakh.

Proposal has been moved to the Government of India for financing the above schemes. The Ministry of Finance, Government of India has released Rs.26.02 crores being 80% grants and 20 % loan of the amount of Rs. 36.58 crores

Deficits and Debt

Manipur had a fiscal deficit for the years during 1992-93 and 1993-94 and a revenue surplus until 1998-99. The heavy outgo on account of implementation of the Fifth Pay Commission's recommendation in 1999-2000 turned the revenue surplus State into revenue Deficit State. Fiscal deficit rose to an unprecedented level of 22.8 per cent of GSDP in the same year. Until 1998-99, the borrowed resources could be devoted to plan outlay only, but from 1999-2000, with the emergence of revenue deficit, the borrowed resources have been financing the revenue deficit as well. The State has borrowed resources for financing revenue expenditure by Rs. 286 crore in 1999-2000, Rs. 86 crores in 2000-01 and Rs. 161 crores in 2001-02 (Table 3.4).

Capital outlay, being linked to the State's plan size, has a tendency to maintain its level in spite of mounting pressure on available resources. Net lending by the Government, which was modest on average, went up rapidly in 2001-02 and 2002-03. In 1999-2000, impounding arrears in small savings and provident fund account, withrawal from public account and depletion in cash balance financed the huge jump of nearly Rs. 550 crore in the fiscal deficit. In the following year, though the fiscal deficit was brought down to Rs. 234 crore, the State still had to resort to overdraft from the Centre to the tune of Rs. 131 crore. The revenue deficit for 2001-02 and 2002-03 are expected to be lower in nominal terms.

The outstanding debt comprising internal debt, debt on account of loans and advances from centre and small savings and provident fund rose to Rs. 214 crore in 1985-86 to Rs. 2024 crores in 2001-02. As a proportion of GSDP, it rose from 46.2 per cent in 1998-99 to 56.7 per cent in 2000-01, as the arrears of pay following the Fifth Pay Commission's award were impounded in the provident fund amounting to Rs. 275 crore and 61.26 per cent in 2001-02. The composition of debt reveals that the share of internal debt, small savings and provident fund at the expense of the falling share of loans from the Centre.

The chronic problem of fiscal deficit has resulted in severe liquidity problems. The magnitude and the frequency of occurrences of imbalances between receipts and expenses became large for Manipur during 1989-90, and the outstanding Ways and Means Advances (WMA) and overdraft became substantial. The situation deteriorated further in 1991-92, and was eventually retrieved in 1993-94. The situation was of more precarious nature as the State finances has continued in the last two years to increasing rely on the WMA and mounting outstanding balances. For the year 2001-02 and 2002-03 saw a huge amounts of such borrowing from RBI i.e. Rs. 1556.44 crores and Rs. 1328.99 crores respectively. Number of overdraft were 329 days in 2001-02 and 342 days in 2002-03. The problem has become so acute that the State is failing to discharge its regular and routine duties, like payment of wages and salaries, spending adequate amount on O&M, and allocating funds for developmental expenditure under the plan heads. Manipur has used WMA and overdraft, which were meant to be for meeting temporary liquidity mismatches, for meeting its structural deficits. The picture worsen even when the hidden liabilities at the end of March 2001are examined, such as deposit under public account for which matching resources are not available (Rs. 148.9 crores pre-actual), receipts from CSS/CPS/NEC etc. but not spent (Rs. 78.35 crore), backlog of State share for CSS/CPS (Rs. 10.07 crores) and pending liabilities of all departments including purchases of power (Rs. 250 crore) totalling to Rs. 487.35 crores are taken into account. To clear all these and opening deficits, Manipur would have required Rs. 1024.10 crore at the beginning of 2002-03.

Table 4.4
Ways and Means Advances(WMA) from RBI and Centre

(Rs. Crore)

		As on March 31							
		1995	*1996*	*1997*	*1998*	*1999*	*2000*	*2001*	*2002*
Outstanding WMA from									
i).	RBI	—	10.04	5.88	8.00	27.70	28.20	41.80	42.40
ii).	Centre	0.51	0.51	0.51	0.51	0.51	3.51	134.17	2.32
	Sub-Total	0.51	10.55	6.39	8.51	28.21	31.71	175.97	44.72
	Outstanding Shortfall and OD	—	10.44	58.39	204.90	383.27	276.84	400.50	497.86
Total		0.51	20.99	64.78	213.41	411.48	308.55	576.47	542.58

Source: Finance Account, various issues, Government of Manipur.

Finance Commission (FC) awards non-plan grants under Article 275 to the States to fill up the gap between non-plan revenue expenditure and non-plan revenue receipts comprising own tax revenue and other non-plan grants(and not including FC non-plan grants). In this exercise an assessment of the future profile of the items of non-plan revenue expenditure for Manipur were assessed at Rs.651.70 crore in 2000-01, and it was expected to grow to Rs. 886.20 crore by the year 2004-05. The State in its Memorandum submitted to the EFC has predicted its non-plan revenue expenditure at Rs. 974 crore in 2000-01, which were projected to grow to Rs. 1532.40 crore by 2004-05. The difference between the the two estimates was Rs. 322.50 crore for 2000-01. A comparison between the EFC and State's Assessment on non-plan revenue expenditure is shown in the following table.

Table 4.5

Non-Plan Revenue Expenditure - the EFC and the State's Assessment

(Rs. Crore)

	1997-98	*1998-99*	*1999-2000*	*2000-01*	*2001-02*	*2002-03*	*2003-04*	*2004-05*
1. Government of Manipur Forecast	608	1039	921	974	1115	1242	1383	1532
2. EFC Forecast	0	0	0	652	700	953	810	1486
3. Actual	606	608	1090	935	1139	NA	NA	NA
4. Shortfall in Grants (1-2)	NA	NA	NA	322	415	289	573	46

Source: EFC Report; State Memorandum submitted to the EFC.

The Government of Manipur White Paper argues that Manipur has been awarded utterly inadequate funds for maintenance of assets by the EFC. The comparison of the neighboring States on maintenance of assets is shown in the Table 3.7.

Governance

The four pillars of good governance are in general accountability, transparency, predictability and participation. It appears that while none of these can by itself lead to good governance, each is instrumental in achieving the remaining three and all the four together in sound and effective public sector management.

In Manipur, it appears that there is a lot of governance failure on all the four counts. In an environment of insurgency, the failure is particularly pronounced in the area of predictability. The people are not sure as to when and if at all an announced policy will be implemented. The case of repealing prohibition- that cost the government a substantial amount of revenue while encouraging the liquor mafia - provides a good example. Prohibition, in spite of being repealed by a Cabinet decision twice in the last couple of years and even after the newly enacted Manipur Liquor Prohibition (Amendment Bills) on July 30, 2002, no concrete steps have been taken to legalise liquor distribution and appoint vendors.

Corruption, which is intricately linked with the concept of good governance, also flourishes in a situation of civil strife. Corruption can be defined as misuse of public and private office for personal gain. As Campo and Sundaram argue (2001) that corruption is increasingly seen all over the world as neither beneficial ("grease for the machine"), inevitable ("the way the system works"), nor respectable ("everybody does it"). Corruption can undermine the credibility of the public sector badly in the eyes of the public, lead to the failure of any good initiative, or a programme, if not suitably designed. The ineffectiveness of government expenditure in Manipur suggests a high degree of misutilization of funds through leakages because of corruption. Some instances of Poor Governance in Manipur are:

- As on March 2001, 5 (five) of the Government Companies in which Government had invested Rs. 10.35 crore, were incurring losses. While the interest on market borrowing during the year was 12 per cent, the investment in Government Companies fetched no returns (Para 1.1 to 1.12).
- Transmission and Distribution (T & D)/Commercial losses in the power sector were Rs. 4.38 crore during 2000-01.
- Though the power tariff was revised in March 2000, the collection was Rs. 26.33 crores (Finance Account 2000-01, Government of Manipur). There was a shortfall of Rs. 25.60 crores against a target of collection of Rs.51.93 crores as power tariff during 2000-01 (Para 3.2) and and the collection was reduced to Rs. 19.73 crore during 2001-02 (Finance Account 2001-02, Government of Manipur).
- Only 3 lawyers out of 903 lawyers registered with the All Manipur Layers Association and High Court Bar Association paid Professional Tax during 2000-01.
- The schemes of Accelerated Urban Water Supply Programmes(AUWSP) were taken up without conducting any survey so as to ascertain number of urban poor families requiring special attention. Out of 15 selected towns, the department identified 6 towns only on the priority list without considering the problems of drinking water faced by the communities. Against a target of 11 schemes covering 1,10,013 population (1991 census), 5 schemes covering population of 33,790 could be executed during 1996-97 to 2000-01.

- 16 road and bridge works taken up before 1995-96 remained incomplete as of March 2001, even after expending Rs. 4.32 crore as of March 2001.
- Closure of 14 incomplete works (due for completion between March, 1991 and March, 1997) led to expenditure of Rs. 1.69 crore incurred on them unproductive.
- Mechnical Division-I incurred expenditure of Rs. 2.46 crores on maintenance of 155 excess staff over the sanctioned strength.
- The Department paid Rs. 14.44 crore to the muster roll and work charged staff in excess of the norms of Rs. 30 per cent of maintenance allocation (Para 4.2).
- Non-completion of RE works in 227 villages resulted in locking up of borrowed funds amounting to 25.47 crore with consequential interest liability of Rs. 5.13 crore.
- Due to slow progress/non-execution of special category schemes, there was locking up of Rs. 9.74 crore resulting in fruitless liability of of interest of Rs. 1.31 crore per annum (Para 8.13).
- Of the 5 loss incurring working companies, aggregate loss incurred by 3 working companies was Rs. 4.33 crore and that by the working corporation was Rs. 16.70 crore.

[*Source:* Report of the Comptroller and Auditor General of India for the year ended March 31, 2001, Government of Manipur.]

Local Bodies

In Manipur, there has been limited progress in decentralization to the third tier. The State Finance Commission was first constituted in April 1994, which was reconstituted in May 1996. The Report was submitted in

December 1996. It was recommended that 5.23 per cent of the State's share in Central Taxes would be devolved to the local bodies. The Government has accepted the recommendations. In a State with rich tradition of good village level governance, this development has to be seen in the context of the ethnic diversity and conflict.

In order to ensure that the State's tax receipts are able to exceed the target set in the MTFRP and ability of the Local Bodies to perform their functions is enhanced, the statutory controls, if any, on the ability of the Local Bodies to take decisions on appropriate level of property tax and profession taxes will be removed and such bodies will be nudged to venture for higher resource mobilization in exercise of such statutory powers. The concerned Administrative Departments will also review the potential and efforts of the Local Bodies, fix annual targets of revenue and monitor their progress on a continual basis.

5

Suggestion for Fiscal Reform

The State needs to take immediate steps to overcome the fiscal crisis by curtailing and rationalizing expenditure and mobilizing more resources, otherwise the existing deficiency in resource is likely to worsen. Steps are also needed for defining Government and reducing its role in direct employment creation. The focus of expenditure restructuring should be on improving the effectiveness of the Government in delivery of public goods and services. The State should also be undertaking measures to create substantial employment opportunities, but in the private sector, through creation of a business-friendly atmosphere, providing a skilled, healthy and educated work force produced by a good education and health system, and building up a good physical infrastructure with facilities such as roads, water supply, power and the most important sector is to facilitate the irrigation to the farmers.

The Memorandum of Understanding (MOU) signed by the Government of Manipur with the Government of India on April 19, 1999 envisaged a host of steps to augment revenue from tax and non-tax sources, reduce revenue expenditure and rein in debt levels, ensure recycling of funds and improve overall transparency and efficiency of governance. Earlier additional resource mobilization and austerity measures had already been introduced, although not with much success. The MoU of 1999 was in the context of the Incentive Fund created under the State's Fiscal Reform Facility on the recommendation of the EFC. Progress in reaching the goals was, patchy at best. A second MoU signed on June 20, 2002 contained a Medium Term Fiscal Restructuring Policy (MTFRP) for 2000-05, and an Empowered Monitoring Committee to oversee progress. Poor implementation of ambitious plans appears to be at the root of these aborted reforms.

The various measures mooted in the First MoU of the State Government did not achieve the desired result because though the expenditure reducing measures were initiated, which entailed major legislative changes could not be initiated with the State under President's Rule (PR). The PR ended only in June 2002. The newly elected Government that replace PR has taken some measures like lifting of prohibition by introducing the Prohibition Bill in July 2002. However, prohibition in effect continues because the Government still has not come out with the necessary notification for giving liquor vendors the licences to open the shops. Furthermore, reforms in major areas, such as downsizing of the Government with significant impact on the State's finances, are still awaited. Another major achievement of the Government were closing down of the identified loss making State Level Public Enterprises (SLPE). The mistakes of the past, when elected Governments failed to implement carefully drawn up plans of reforms, but also a persistent implementation strategy of plans. The new Government with its popular mandate is ideally placed to extricate the State out of the current morass of fiscal paralysis.

Issues of Policy and Management

The trends in government's finances, as summarized

above, raise a large number of micro issues relating to both the policy as well as management of Debt, Resources and Expenditure.

Debt

The nominal stock of domestic debt of the combined Government sector has been growing at a rate of about 43 per cent during the later part of the 1990s. At the end of March 2002, the stock of domestic debt was 61 per cent of GSDP. As high level of public debt have deleterious effects on macroeconomic stability, the need for reducing the fiscal deficit and debt to sustainable levels through institution of policy oriented fiscal rules is widely felt (RBI 2000, August). On the management of public debt, the issues are to minimized the cost of borrowing and to avoid concentration of debt towards the shorter end leading to bunching of redemption and roll over problems. The RBI and the Department of Economic Affairs, the Ministry of Finance has a joint committee to regularly review the management of debt operations and status.

Resources Mobilisation

Rising of resources through taxes is a complex and long-term policy issue for any Government. The tax revenue, among other things, is mainly linked to the developments in the real economy. Major policy decisions have to be taken considering a large number of theoretical principles of equity, progressivity and also the considerations of political pragmatism.

On the management side, the administrative reforms including modernization of the tax collection system is the most critical task for the government.

The policy on non-tax revenue, including returns on investments made in the public sector enterprises, has been an issue of wide debate in the economy. However, it is the management of the process of disinvestments, privatization and restructuring of PSUs, which is found to be most critical.

Proper Collection Mechanism

Hike of user charges should be accompanied with a proper mechanism of collection and quality of services. Collection of user charges is poor in Manipur (C & AG 2001).

There is a need for considering innovative solutions for improving collections. In the case of Electricity, this is already in place with one such innovative solution for the Government employees. The Government employees now have to produce no-due certificates every six months while getting their salaries. The system could be extended to the other user charges such as water, particularly in view of the large size of Government employment in Manipur. Furthermore, the State can consider privatizing the collection of user charge, either by private bodies or local clubs on a commission basis. This will also facilitate the downsizing of various departments and economy on the wage-bill of the Government.

Revenue for Local Bodies

Local bodies, both in urban as well as in rural areas, are the best agencies for supplying the local public good such as town or village roads, street lighting and sewerage. Apart from the transfers from the State Government, they need to mobilize their own revenues to augment their resources and to develop a sence of ownership, accountability and responsibility. Octroi or an entry tax, specially when it is based on physical stoppage and verification of goods movement, tend to slow down traffic on already congested and badly maintain roads, and lead to corruption. Hence the possibility of levy of such tax by local bodies should await the introduction of computerization of the sales tax department and introduction of VAT, when such a tax can be efficiently levied on an accounts-basis. In the meantime, the house or property tax, user charges for services such as sanitation, and maintenance of street lighting and fees on daily or weekly markets should be bolstered.

House / Property Tax

At present there is no house or property tax in urban areas. The local urban bodies should be empowered to collect a house/property tax. The tax should be based on the unit area method. The house/property tax will not only be a source of revenue, but will also provide the basis of providing civic services to the people, including the maintenance of the places of pilgrimages. The levying of house tax should be accompanied by a phasing out of the Rent Control Act to avoid owners paying the tax while tenants continue to pay low rents at historic rates in even relatively better-off localities.

Service Charges

The municipalities/local bodies should levy services, such as, sanitation and maintenance of street lighting. It may be useful to have a State-wide law for the compulsory levy of such charges to begin with. By avoiding a popular race to the bottom of having low or no user charges, this will help develop the "user pays" principle in local bodies. With time, as the system get entrenched, the State law can be repealed to give local bodies additional flexibility to fix their appropriate level of service as well as charges to suit local tastes and preferences.

Levying of Fees on Daily / Weekly Markets

The local government should levy nominal fees on the daily/weekly markets, which may be utilized for better maintenance of market places, including the women-dominated small retail markets. Provision of civic amenities to these markets will mobilize popular support for such a fee on daily/weekly markets.

Expenditure Reform

It is the expenditure policy, which in the ultimate sense is responsible for the success or failure of the whole fiscal stance. It is not the allocation of budgetary resources, alone which matter, but there is a larger issue of state policy, effective governance and impact of the expenditure, which assumes importance.

Expenditure policy in fact has to pursue all the general objectives of macroeconomic policy: growth, stability and equity. The performance of the state policy at the end of the day is measure only in terms of effectiveness of public expenditure, efficiency of resource use and responsive system.

The Need of Expenditure Management

Lahiri, Ashok K. has suggested, "Expenditure management through appropriate priotisation and control is important for any Government. The tension between the deficit and providing adequate outlays for the relevant heads makes expenditure prioritization an even more important issue in India than what it is in many other countries. There is need for more schools, hospitals, roads, hydroelectric and multipurpose irrigation projects etc. on the one hand, and sticking to fiscal prudence on the other. One of the traditional ways of safeguarding the fiscal balance is through a strict adherence to appropriate budgeting techniques and procedures.

Announce a VRS Package Identical to that of the Government of India

An employee separated under VRS will give rise to a different stream of out-payments than the stream when she continues in service. Under VRS, the Government saves the salary and wages, together with the other allowances, that it would have had to pay for the rest of her employment period until the normal retirement age of 58. But, on the other hand, the Government has to pay to termination benefits of gratuity and leave encashment amount upfront upon voluntary retirement. Furthermore, it also has to pay the ex-gratia amount eligible under VRS. While no salary is payable in the future, pension, if applicable, together with any commutation of the same, also becomes payable earlier from the date of voluntary retirement.

Using alternative assumptions for inflation correction, rate of interest and increments to salary, it can be shown that VRS represents lower net present value for all cases with less than 4 years of employment left. However, there is an adverse impact on state finances in the short run, and a loan would be necessary to finance the scheme. Under reasonable assumption of 10 per cent interest, it can be shown that a loan of the amount equivalent to the lump sum VRS payment could be serviced–including repayment–out of savings generated from wages and salaries, inclusive of all likely increases resulting from inflation correction and increments, of the relieved employees, in five years, and from the sixth year onwards, create fiscal space for additional expenditure.

The responsibility of identifying surplus staff should be entrusted to the respective departments, and the surplus staff, who are above 50 years of age, should be told that they would be discharged from their positions in case they do not opt for the VRS under Rule 56J.

Power

Given the importance of power as a universal input, it is critical that the sector is put on an accelerated reform path. With no State Electricity Board, the state electricity department looks after the power sector. Since August 1984, the Loktak Hydro Electric Project is the main source of power supply in the State. The State has assigned the task of preparing a report on power sector reform to the Administrative Staff College of India (ASCI), Hyderabad.

While full-scale power sector reform has to await the ASCI report, the reform actions contained in the MOU between GOI and the Government of Manipur of June 20, 2002, including the clearing of dues from various government departments and autonomous bodies, should be fully implemented. The potentials of power generation from Tipaimukh Project, Loktak Down Stream Project, Tuivai Hydro Electric Project and micro-hydel schemes should be reviewed.

Agriculture and Irrigation

The mainstay of Manipur being agriculture, the dependence on single crop agriculture has to be reduced through better irrigation facilities. There must be emphasis on the exotic variety of lily, sandalwood, ginger, turmeric, and orange plantations. The hills of Manipur are highly suitable for the development of horticulture, and the possibility of leasing out lands to companies with wide distribution network at an appropriate price should be considered. This of course will be successful only when insurgency is brought under control. The issue of land ownership, a very sensitive issue, should be de-politicized through an informed public debate.

Index

■■■